THE OTHER SIDE OF LIFE

THE OTHER SIDE OF LIFE

GAIN A POSITIVE PERSPECTIVE AND SEE LIFE MORE CLEARLY

Go to **michaelunks.com**
To get the first five chapters of the
audio book for free.

MICHAEL UNKS

Thank you for checking out this book.

I'm providing you the first five chapters of the audio version of this book for free.
Click the link below:

Send me the audio book

Also check out michaelunks.com for more free audio books!

I also have several book ideas. I can let you know when my next one comes out by clicking below:

Keep me posted

TABLE OF CONTENTS

CHAPTER 1

INTRODUCTION TO THE OTHER SIDE OF LIFE

I got the idea for this book from my ninth-grade trigonometry class. I honestly don't even remember my teacher's name, but I do remember a quiz that forever changed my life. The class was right before lunch and all I cared about was getting one of the three-dollar mega meals that were always quickly claimed. If you weren't the first 30 in line, you weren't getting the mega meal. Instead, you had to settle for the standard meal.

The standard meal was $1.75 and didn't suit my fancy. Beef stroganoff, shepherd's pie, or meatloaf. *Yuck, no thank you.* Sometimes the standard meal was decent, like the days of corn dogs or chicken nuggets. But no matter what, the mega meal reigned supreme.

The mega meal was a fried chicken sandwich that tasted like it came from Chick-Fil-A, a giant rectangular basket full of fries that tasted like the fries from McDonald's, and a Styrofoam cup of shaved ice, which you could fill unlimited times with sweet tea. All of that for *only* three dollars. What a deal!

Lunch period started at 1 p.m. Two minutes before, I would make sure to get into a sprinter's stance to be the first out of that trigonometry class.

Clearly, my focus wasn't on trigonometry, which caused an error on the quiz. I didn't think about that quiz in the ten years since that class, but this past year, I've been obsessed with it.

I knew I would get a 100. The questions were easy. I was rushing to finish as fast as I could and show off to my teacher how smart I was. Plus, by finishing early I would secure what mattered most to me: my mega meal for the day.

I was completely dumbfounded when the teacher returned my quiz the following class period. The grade of a 50 was written in red ink on the top right corner. *What happened?* I was certain every question was right.

The thing is, I *did* get every question I answered right, yet still failed. How could this be?

I only answered the front side of the quiz. *I did not answer the other side of it.* I went to the teacher assuming she would let me answer the other side, but she said no. I found her response annoying and unfair, but it wasn't a big deal. It was just a quiz. It's not like it was a test. Plus, staying after class to argue with her would prevent me enjoying that mega meal. Nothing was getting in my way of me and that mega meal. *Nothing.*

Time has passed, and I've learned there is more to life than having a fantastic meal. At the very least, I hoped there was. Is life like that two-sided quiz and we aren't answering the other side of it?

That quiz started turning my gears. It made me realize that you could be failing in life, not because you're not putting in the work or because you're lacking the ability to supply the right answers, but because you're missing the other side. The side you won't see until you start looking for it.

Maybe you feel like you're doing all the right things. You go to the gym and put in the effort to look physically attractive. You go to college, get a fancy degree, and from that a solid career. You may be constantly setting goals and achieving them. But these goals only make you feel temporarily fulfilled. You still find yourself asking, "Is this it?" after accomplishing them.

I believe life *is* like that two-sided quiz, and there's another side that we aren't answering. There is a life of pleasure on the front, but there is also a life of purpose on the back. You can stay on the front side of life like me, trying to find fulfillment in pleasures of a fried chicken sandwich, French fries, and sweat tea. Sure, it can feel amazing in the short run, but it will never sustain you long term.

The Other Side of Life is about living a life of purpose. It is about learning all the lessons life has to teach you and then sharing what you have with others. The other side of life is less concerned about a comfortable life, but rather a life of character. A life of learning, growing, and contributing your gifts to the world to make it a better place.

Over the years, I've made the effort to turn to the other side in my life, hoping to answer questions I've missed. I've made the effort to surround myself with wise people to teach me all that I had to learn about life, which, as it turns out, is *a lot*.

The price you have to pay may be more than three dollars, but I promise that looking at the other side of life will bring you long-lasting fulfillment. It will be a deal infinitely better than that three-dollar mega meal.

If you turn to the back of the paper first and answer those questions, you'll then be able to turn back to the front and answer those questions, too. Only this time, you now give yourself a chance to be able to answer *all* of life's questions and ace its test. *The Other Side* is much deeper and more fulfilling. In fact, since turning to the other side, my burning desire for shallow pleasures like that mega meal in ninth grade don't consume me the way they used to.

Look at the top part of your hand. The top part is what you can see. It's what's happening in your life. However, when you turn your hand over you see the other side of your hand, a side you couldn't see moments ago. It's the same with reflection and seeking to learn from your failures. You see lessons from life that could truly change your life, and insights that you were previously not able to see.

If you feel like you're scoring a 50 in life, it's likely there's a side you're not even seeing, a side you're not answering. There's no need to worry, though. If someone like me can see the other side of life and overcome his failures, I know you can, too.

Your life means more than a ninth grade math quiz. My teacher didn't let me go back and answer the other side of that quiz. The good news is that my unreasonable teacher doesn't hold the power over us to go back and answer the other side of our lives. You can turn your life over *right now* and start enjoying the parts of life you've been missing.

The question is, *will* you? This book contains dozens of unique stories that will forever change how you see life. This book will show you how to take moments in your life and ask yourself questions you don't normally ask to get positive results you wouldn't expect.

Let me show you how to gain a positive perspective and see life more clearly. Let me show you what the other side of life looks like.

CHAPTER 2

WHAT DO YOU SEE?

Imagine someone you admire and respect coming up to you and saying, "I see greatness in you. You have tremendous potential and I can't wait to see what your future holds." They aren't trying to flatter you or get something out of you. They genuinely believe in you. This person has a vision for your life that would excite you and cause you to start working towards that vision, or it may have *absolutely no effect on you at all.*

It all depends on *your* vision. Years ago a mentor of mine was giving me vague phrases of encouragement such as "you have a bright future" and "you have tremendous potential" and it felt great. A couple years went by and I ran into this mentor again and he asked what I had been up to.

I told him about the hundreds of book ideas that I had. I think I spent over an hour sharing stories, ideas, and metaphors that would cause people to think about themselves and their world differently.

He responded, "Where can I buy this book with all these ideas?" With a tone of disappointment I responded, "You can't buy it. There is no book. I guess I'm all talk." What he told me is what I'm going to tell you. If you're not where you'd like to be in your life, the biggest problem isn't that you aren't capable or lacking motivation. The problem is that you're lacking vision.

Without vision, you might be filled with amazing ideas and dreams, but you are unable to make any progress on making them a reality. I remind myself of the troubles Helen Keller had to deal with. She was deaf *and* blind. Imagine not being able to hear *or* see anything. I have quiet time in the morning where I close my eyes and put in ear plugs, but I do it for twenty minutes. Helen Keller had to do it her whole life.

But Helen Keller has said, "The only thing worse than being blind is having sight, but no vision." *Wow!* There are many aspects to your vision that need to be corrected in order to reach your highest potential. You start with the way you see yourself. I suppose we choose to see ourselves in a lower light so people don't think we're arrogant and full of ourselves. Maybe we do it to rob ourselves of hope, because that hope would lead to action, and what if those actions lead to disappointment? Whatever your reason, let's address the artist in your mind.

In 2013, the soap company Dove created a series of short films with women and an FBI-trained forensic artist. Without seeing the women, the artist drew each woman according to how she saw herself. Later, the artist drew that same woman based on how a stranger described her. The results were surprising. The sketches drawn from the stranger's description were always more beautiful than the ones where the women described themselves.

The campaign helped show that complete strangers may have a higher opinion of you than you have of yourself. You may not be a woman who is struggling to see the beauty in yourself, but we all have a forensic artist in our mind, drawing out how we describe ourselves. If you're unwilling to describe yourself and your future in a brighter way, you risk missing out on opportunities that are already present in your life.

A mentor and close friend of mine was trying to convey how not having a better vision of yourself leads to regret. He shared a time when he was 18. He pulled up a picture on his Facebook page and showed me a woman who was somewhat attractive for her age and asked, "What do you think of her?" Trying to be funny I replied, "She's beautiful, but possibly a tad bit too old for me." He laughed and then continued, "This is Ms. Georgia. In 1977 she was considered the most beautiful woman in the entire state."

He then brought up a picture of "Ms. Georgia" when she was in her twenties. Her beauty had me speechless. I modified the year and state, so you won't find this woman, but the story is still real. He continued, "I've gotten better looking over the years, but you would not believe how I looked when I was 18. One of the ugliest guys you'd ever see."

He pulled up a high school picture of himself, and just like the women in that Dove campaign, he was seeing himself worse than what others were seeing. He had pale skin and curly red hair, but if you were to look at his photo you'd likely consider him average to slightly-above-average in looks. "Ms. Georgia" had just moved to my friend's high school and they were next-door neighbors.

She didn't know anybody and asked my friend to show her around. Several times a week they would go to different restaurants, work on homework assignments for several hours after school, and go to the movies on the weekend. While sharing these moments my friend had a big grin on his face. "It was the most exciting three months of my life. I didn't know why a girl like this wanted to spend time with a guy like me, but I was grateful she wanted to be friends with me."

Then one day Ms. Georgia said to him, "We need to talk about something that's been on my mind for awhile. Please be honest with me." Puzzled, he responded, "I'll be honest with you. What is it?" In a more serious tone she asked, "Are you attracted to me?" He immediately shot back, "What?! Of course I'm attracted to you. What makes you think that I'm not?"

Her answer displays my friend's vision problem. "We've been dating for three months and not *once* have you even tried to kiss me." You see, my friend thought so lowly of himself that he couldn't believe a girl like Ms. Georgia would see him as anything more than a friend. He had lots of wonderful qualities: he was kind, generous, had a fantastic sense of humor, was brilliant, and was a gentleman. Ms. Georgia could see it, but my friend couldn't. My friend missed out on a great opportunity due to the artist in his mind.

Reflect on this quote by Dr. Joyce Brothers so you don't make the mistake my friend made; "You cannot consistently perform in a manner which is inconsistent with how you see yourself." Hundreds of people share their aspirations with me and I constantly find myself thinking, *why are they not doing it?* They could be beyond qualified for the promotion they want, but they refuse to submit an application for it. Why? Because they don't see themselves as a person making that salary or having that type of responsibility.

You may be a gifted painter, writer, singer, or have an idea that could become a successful business, but you never seriously pursue it. Why? Because you see it as a fantasy. You're unable to envision someone reaching into their wallet and paying you to share your gifts with them. Or you could be waiting for someone to give you an opportunity. Maybe you think, *If someone would just give me a chance I would wow them!*

My friend, you're likely not making progress not because others aren't giving you a chance, but because you're not giving *yourself* a chance. You see, my friend told me this story about Ms. Georgia years ago, and the moral was that someone could see something in you, but you wouldn't go anywhere until you gave yourself a chance to see it, too.

Sometimes you have to evaluate your approach, and if it's not working, simply change it. Focusing on your flaws, failures, and fumbles is not the answer. If you're like me, having high aspirations for life, but at times struggling to make progress on them, consider this advice from author Louise Hay, "Remember, you have been criticizing yourself for years. And it hasn't worked. Try approving of yourself and see what happens."

You can start approving of yourself and your abilities, but still not progress in life the way you'd like. It could be because we spend too much time visualizing the end results and not the process. There's an unfortunate truth about this process that I wish wasn't true. I learned this truth from a faulty faucet in a hotel a couple months back.

I had a terrific night's sleep at a Holiday Inn Express and woke up the following morning eager to start my day. I hopped into the shower and turned the shower handle to the middle. It was scalding hot. I moved it slightly to the right. Now it was so cold that it was giving me goosebumps. I moved it slightly back to the left, and it was scalding hot again. With no exaggeration, I must have spent five minutes adjusting the shower handle ever so slightly and it kept going from piping hot to ice cold.

I had accepted that if I wanted to shower that day and make it to work on time, I would have to take the shower with a temperature that was uncomfortable for me. Outside the shower issue, I had a delightful time at that Holiday Inn Express and highly recommend you stay there if you're looking for a classy room and a great rate.

We all have different shower temperature preferences, but that morning, the medium temperature I preferred was not an option. It was either shower uncomfortably, or don't shower at all. So many times with our dreams and goals, we are enthusiastic about pursuing them, but we often don't work on them until we find our preferred conditions, like our preferred shower temperature.

Maybe we're waiting until we are feeling motivated to do something. Maybe we're waiting until our fears go away. Maybe we're waiting until we are confident in our abilities. Maybe we wait until the first of the year. Maybe we wait until we have enough money saved up. Whatever it is, we wait for ideal conditions to start working on something.

Life is like that faulty faucet; it's trying to test you. There are going to be moments in your life where you will not be able to have the ideal conditions no matter how hard you try. There are going to be moments in your life where you'll have the option of piping hot or ice cold. These are moments that test your commitment and display the confidence in your vision. Vision is about faith. It's about seeing something in your mind that you can't currently see and acting on it to bring it into reality. Are you willing to show up and put in the work, even when it's not convenient, even when you're tired and scared, and even when you aren't motivated?

We often make the mistake of hearing a success story where something happened for that person very fast and we believe it will happen to us too. For example, I heard that Sylvester Stallone wrote the screenplay for *Rocky* in 20 hours, and I was hoping I could sit down in one day and write something valuable, too.

After years of talking about writing a book and not writing a single sentence, I was motivated after hearing about Sylvester Stallone's success. I chugged two zero-calorie Orange Sunrise Monster energy drinks and sat down at my desk to write a masterpiece. An hour went by and I had *nothing*. Another hour went by and my excitement started to fade. After four hours, I had only a few paragraphs that I eventually erased because it wasn't worth sharing.

I decided to take a break and come back to the book when I was feeling motivated. But I never felt motivated. Several months went by before I realized my view on the process was setting me up to fail.

Yes, it's possible to strike lightning in a bottle and come up with an idea in a short period of time like Sylvester Stallone did with *Rocky*.

But stories like this are the exception, not the rule. For the majority of all success stories, they involved people showing up to work when they didn't feel like it. They involved people trying and failing countless times until they finally got it right or when they finally got the opportunity. I've changed my expectations on the process and it's helped me make progress with many goals. Writing this book is one of them.

I'm learning that in order to bring your vision to pass, you'll have to work on it when you don't feel like it. Many days it won't come easy to you and many days you won't feel like it. Just like that day in the shower, it came to a point where I had to get over the temperature and accomplish my mission, which was taking a shower. Just like you have to get over your discomfort and doubts to accomplish your mission.

I realized that if I wanted to write a book, I would need to sit down and start writing, even when I wasn't certain what to write about. However, I understood that uncertainty and doubt would be part of the process. I also chose to believe that with patience and persistence, life lessons would emerge that would help you live a better life. Also, I told the artist in my mind that doubt and discomfort would be part of the process and to not let that distort the picture of bringing the vision to pass.

There are dozens of stories where I sat down for hours writing them out, but then realized they weren't good. I tossed them out. There are other stories I rewrote over a dozen times to get them to where they were clear and helpful. If I didn't get an accurate vision, and if I didn't expect this extra work as part of the process, I would have lost patience and given up. Since these struggles are now part of my vision, when the struggles come, they don't derail me.

It's just part of being human. You want to do the things that you're excited about, make you comfortable, and come easy to you. You don't want to do the things that are boring, make you uncomfortable, and are hard. But when you're seeing the positive aspects of yourself, and your vision of the process is realistic, you will be more likely to fulfill your grand visions.

Let me show you something you'll never forget.

According to research at Cambridge University, it deosn't mttaer in waht oredr the ltteers in a wrod are, the olny iprmoatnt tihng is taht the frist and lsat ltteer be at the rghit pclae. The rset can be a toatl mses and you can sitll raed it wouthit a porbelm. Tihs is bcuseae the huamn mnid deos not raed ervey lteter by istlef, but the wrod as a wlohe.

Were you able to understand the previous paragraph? That's why vision is so important. When you're clear on who you are, where you are, and what you're about, that's like your first letter. When you have a vision for who you're becoming, and where you're going, that's like the last letter. The middle letters that are jumbled up represent your life. It never seems to go the way you planned, and often times it's tough to make sense of it.

Whenever you find yourself in a rut, experiencing a setback, or experiencing a nonsense word in your life, don't give up and close the book on your life's story. Keep moving forward. You may not believe it, but your vision helps you understand the jumbled words of your life story. Use the examples of this chapter to add clarity to your vision.

I can see greatness in you, but will you be brave enough to see it in yourself? Will you tell the artist in your mind to paint a masterpiece of what your future holds and who you're becoming, or will you tell it awful things to avoid the risk of disappointment? Also, learn from that faulty faucet. Sometimes in life you won't be able to have the temperature that's most comfortable for you, but that's by design.

Doing it when it's not ideal develops character and displays commitment. When you're showing up no matter what, that is when you give yourself the best chance of letting others see your grandest visions. Apply what you learn in this chapter and I believe the world will see the other side of you, the side that inspires us all.

CHAPTER 3

ETCH-A-SKETCH ARTISTS

The Etch-A-Sketch is a wildly popular toy. According to CNBC, more than 100 million Etch-A-Sketches have been sold since its introduction in 1960. I wasn't a big fan. I found it almost impossible to maneuver the knobs to even create a circle. Silly putty was more enjoyable. Less skill and thinking required.

Since I was never able to draw anything of value, I didn't have the fear others had of someone taking their masterpiece, shaking it, and within seconds erasing it. Google "Etch-A-Sketch art" and you'll find some gifted artists who have spent a considerable amount of time honing their craft on the popular red, rectangular toy. Etchings of the Mona Lisa, Taj Mahal, and The Beatles will mesmerize you.

It's hard to grasp why someone would spend so much time creating their art on a device that isn't meant to be permanent. Why risk having your image shaken and erased completely? Imagine spending months drawing your own version of the Mona Lisa. Everyone who sees it is in awe of your creative genius. The art is good. Too good. It causes people to become jealous and want to shake your work away. You could also shake your own work away. All it takes is one moment of clumsiness to drop your Etch-A-Sketch and ruin your art. What causes you to drop it? You respond to a text? You didn't nail your art to the wall properly? Greasy fingers due to a large order of curly fries from Arby's?

It turns out the pros know how to make their work permanent. One Etch-A-Sketch artist, Nicole Falzone, is often referred to as the "Monet of the Magic Screen" for her intricate portraits of celebrities like Stevie Wonder, Bill Gates, and Albert Einstein. She shared her secret. To make her etchings permanent she drills holes in the back of the casing to drain the Etch-A-Sketch of its aluminum powder. In doing so, the lines won't be erased.

To keep your art permanent on the Etch-A-Sketch, you have to destroy it. You have two options if you're an aspiring artist that doesn't want your image to be shaken. You can either remove the powder from the Etch-A-Sketch and ruin the toy, or create your art on another canvas.

The problem you may be having in your life is that your identity is being drawn on the proverbial Etch-A-Sketch. Maybe things are great in your life, but all it takes is something or someone to shake your picture, taking your work of art and transforming it into an image more disappointing than one of my Etch-A-Sketch drawings. Think of comments that you've received from others over the years. You can likely recall some great moments such as your mom, dad, friend, or significant other saying they believe in you and you can do whatever you set your mind to. Unfortunately, you also can recall negative comments. Those negative ones likely had a more profound effect on you, too.

Back in the day you were less likely to hear the negative criticism hurled your way. However, with the internet, people have an avenue to be more critical and cruel. This negative criticism has the potential to shake your positive image, or to etch over a negative one if you're operating on a proverbial Etch-A-Sketch.

Let's live through the lens of a first-year college professor, Dr. D. Let's say he has a heart for molding young minds. He's spent close to ten years earning his PhD, and landed his dream job at his alma mater.

On the surface, everything seems to be going well for the first semester. The class laughs at his jokes, students seem incredibly interested in what he's teaching, and his picture can't be more perfect. His first semester is over. He's receiving hugs, high-fives, and gift baskets from many students. His confidence is at an all-time high, because he's doing what he loves and is excelling at it. A fellow professor notices the pep in the man's step and comments, "When I started out I felt the same way. Then I found out about ratemyprofessors.com and students' rotten comments destroyed my confidence."

Dr. D's curiosity gets the best of him, and he decides to log onto the website to see what people are saying about him. The site, ratemyprofessors.com, provides one of the best college professor reviews and ratings source based on student feedback. As of 2019, there's over 1.7 million professors & 19 million reviews.

Dr. D logs onto the site and sees that his students wrote 112 reviews. He goes through them and is loving what he sees. "Dr. D is my hero. I want to be just like him someday." "Dr. D took a subject I was dreading and made it my favorite class I've ever taken. Plus, he's hilarious." "Incredibly entertaining and knowledgeable professor. Oh, and let's not forget he's a total stud muffin." The last comment is irrelevant to his teaching and a tad inappropriate, but he's flattered nonetheless.

He's happy that he chose to check out his reviews, because they are making the picture he has of himself more beautiful than ever before. Remember, Dr. D. received 112 reviews. There had to be a brutal comment coming. In fact, he receives three reviews that have the potential to override the 109 glowing ones.

The following three reviews are *real* reviews left by students for *real* professors. We're living through the lens of Dr. D. Imagine how he would take these comments: "Bring a pillow to class so when you lose consciousness your head won't slam on your desk. And bring a pillow for your pillow because your pillow will fall asleep too." Dr. D thinks, *My hat is off to this student for their wittiness, but ouch! No big deal though. It's just one comment. I won't let it get to me.* He discovers another negative one, "I don't wear my seatbelt driving to school because I want to die before I can make it to his class." *Okay, now this student is taking this too far. He or she is just trying to be funny.* Now that he's received two negative reviews, Dr. D's confidence is shaken. He's focusing on all the positive reviews like the one where a student said he was his hero and wants to be like him. He's more confident, but still a little shaken. He's even reminding himself that someone thinks he's a stud muffin. Reflecting on this flattering, yet inappropriate review seems to completely restore his confidence.

But he's yet to read the third negative review. This third review is going to test him. It will not only test Dr. D's image of himself as a teacher, but as a person as well. "He seems happy, and teaches well, but there's something off about him that I can't put my finger on. He smiles, but there's no warmth there. Just a terrible emptiness like you'd find in the rusting hull of a ship forgotten at the bottom of the Dead Sea. Something happened to him to make him this way. I do not know what it was. No one does." Dr. D reads the review again because he cannot believe what he just read. He's letting this comment get to his head. *I have no warmth in my smile?* He looks in the mirror to evaluate his smile. Over the winter break he asks dozens of people if his smile has warmth behind it.

Everyone says they see warmth, but Dr. D isn't convinced. He examines that review some more. *An emptiness like a rusted ship at the bottom of the Dead Sea? What is this student talking about? I'm not empty!* Plus, what is making this student think that something happened to me? Nothing happened to me! The last part of the review, "no one does," seems to be having the largest effect on him because Dr. D is now concerned that students are talking with each other and they all feel the same way.

By now, Dr. D has spent three weeks dwelling on these three negative reviews. He has allowed these comments to shake his positive image of himself, and is image is now been replaced. He now sees a man so boring that he not only puts students to sleep, but their pillows as well. He now sees a man who is so unpleasant that students are driving without their seatbelts, hoping to tragically escape having to spend three hours a week with him. He now sees a man lacking warmth and a man full of emptiness like you'd find in a rusted ship on the bottom of the Dead Sea.

It's widely accepted by psychologists that we project to others the image we have of ourselves. Dr. D used to be a warm, enthusiastic studmuffin. Now he projects a cold, boring, rusted ship you'd find at the bottom of the Dead Sea.

Semester two is drastically different. He dreads teaching class, he cuts down his social time with his friends and family because he believes he burdens them with how boring and empty he is. He is at the lowest point in his life.

He decides it's time to seek wisdom. Dr. D comes across a quote from billionaire Warren Buffett, "You will continue to suffer if you have an emotional reaction to everything that is said to you. True power is observing things with logic. True power is restraint. If words control you that means everyone else can control you. Breathe and allow things to pass." Dr. D takes a breath and allows things to pass. Using his logic, he realizes he had control of his mental Etch-A-Sketch.

He starts to examine the reviews. *Were these reviews helpful? Did they give anything of value that could make me a better teacher?* He immediately answers himself with an emphatic "no!" and ponders why he allowed the comments to have so much power over him these past few months. He then starts to question the motives of the students. *Is it possible these negative comments have nothing to do with me? Is it possible that the students didn't get the grade they were hoping for and used the review as a way to get back at me? Is it possible that they see someone who loves their life and wrote the review to try to make me miserable?*

He believes these are all possible and now has serious doubt if the reviews are even true. Dr. D is now in a more positive state of mind and realizes that he chose to let those negative comments shake his positive image. He chose to let them etch an awful image. Most importantly, he chose to let the image of who he is as a person be drawn on an Etch-A-Sketch.

Once he realized this, he knew that positive reviews could have the same disastrous effect. You see, if Dr. D only focused on what he wanted to hear, he would only accept comments that were glowing. The ones where he's hilarious, confident, and a studmuffin. He knows that how he looks doesn't matter as it pertains to teaching, but he's still flattered by a student out there thinking he's a stud muffin.

As long as Dr. D's image is etched on a mental Etch-A-Sketch, his image will always be based on what comments he chooses to accept. He knows the negative, destructive reviews derail him. He also knows that if he only takes in positive reviews, he'll have an inflated view of himself. He'll also miss out on constructive reviews that will make him a better teacher. For example, one student could say, "He's a great teacher, but at times went on tangents that made it hard for me to get back on track." Dr. D could test this review and have another teacher evaluate him, or he could evaluate himself, to avoid unnecessary tangents. Another student could say, "He was my favorite teacher, but he never seemed to be available during office hours." This review has a simple solution. He realizes the problem here is that during office hours his door is closed, and the *Hootie & the Blowfish* CDs he plays make it seem unwelcoming for students. Dr. D is helped by this review and decides to open his office door during office hours and states to the class that anyone that wants extra help from him will receive it. He'll even turn his *Hootie* jams down while they visit if needed.

Dr. D no longer defines himself using a mental Etch-A-Sketch. He realizes he's a teacher, but he's so much more than that. He's a husband, father, son, friend, and Hootie & the Blowfish fan. He knows the opinions that others have of him are always subject to change. That's why his image is now rooted in his core values. He strives for excellence in all areas of his life. He takes in constructive criticism to improve himself and has the wisdom to discard destructive ones. He is a man of integrity and strives to do the right thing, even when it's the hard thing. He's grateful for everything he has. Being a person of excellence, integrity, and gratitude is something of which you have control. They can be values that are permanent etchings as long as you carry them out with the necessary actions that reflect them.

Because Dr. D no longer uses a mental Etch-A-Sketch, it's extremely difficult to shake his love for molding young minds or his values. In fact, for the rest of his life no event in his life can shake him, and no person's comment can shake him unless he chooses to let it. Maybe a majority of people consider Dr. D a studmuffin. However, his looks are going to eventually fade, but his confidence isn't rooted in his appearance. Your confidence shouldn't be rooted in your profession either because in an instant something could happen to cause you to never perform your work again.

National Geographic interviewed Jeff Gagliardi back in 2012. Jeff had been making and selling Etch-A-Sketch drawings for over 35 years. His etchings were so good people thought he used lasers. However, in 2014, he had an accident where he fell off his roof and broke both his arms at the wrist. This injury put his Etch-A-Sketch days behind him. He might have been known for his Etch-A-Sketch art, but it didn't define him. He is still able to practice his art through painting and does graphic design for a living. He also has a family who loves and supports him with or without his etchings.

At the end of the article, Jeff provides advice for would-be Etch-A-Sketch artists and shares the agony involved in pursuing the craft. "The real secret of it is the ability to retrace a line. And it can be frustrating, as you can imagine. If you mess it up in any way, you just gotta shake it and start all over. There are times when I've gotten right to the end of something and made a mistake, and I'll be honest, you just wanna cry. But hey, if it was easy everyone would be doing it."

Think deeper here. If you want to sharpen your real Etch-A-Sketch skills, embrace it as a fun challenge. As far as using a proverbial Etch-A-Sketch for your self-image, choose another medium for the work of art that represents you. For the artist using an Etch-A-Sketch, everything needs to be perfect from start to finish or it has to be redone. In a similar way, when you are trying to be perfect, to be free of mistakes and to have everyone love you, you'll never etch an image you're satisfied with. Plus, like Dr. D's negative reviews, you'll let destructive criticism shake you and cause you to have to start from scratch. Mistakes will shake you, too. Something as small as forgetting to mail your mom a card for her birthday will cause you to start all over again as well. Dwell on destructive criticism and your mistakes too long, and you'll find yourself etching a negative image that you'll be projecting to the world the rest of your life.

Don't etch your identity on an Etch-A-Sketch. No matter how great you are, there will always be some mistake that you make or one comment someone makes that shakes your precious work of art. Don't identify with what others think of you or what you do. These are not always in your control. Your values are. Be a person who wants to grow, taking in constructive feedback and striving for excellence. Be grateful for who you are and the unique attributes you have to offer the world. By all means try to draw the Mona Lisa on your Etch-A-Sketch. But don't draw your identity on an Etch-A-

Sketch and allow the image to shake you. Instead, shake the world in a positive way by being drawn by your values and character.

CHAPTER 4

YOUR GREAT POWER

Have you ever walked out of a movie and decide you want to be one of the characters? There have been countless times where a guy is shirtless and has an incredible six pack and I think, *I'm going to be built like that guy! Starting tomorrow, no more junk food, nothing but lean meats and vegetables, and I'm going to work out every day.*

The inspiration usually wears off a few hours after the movie. I like the *idea* of having a chiseled physique like Hugh Jackman in the *Wolverine* movies, but don't like the work involved to make that happen. We feel bad for not following through on our goals, so we use our creative brain power to come up with a reason why not making any changes in our lives is okay.

You don't need to be built like Hugh Jackman. Besides, you need people to like you for your personality, not how ripped you are. But, when I was 12 I was inspired after watching the *Spider-Man* movies starring Tobey Maguire. The feeling of wanting to be Spider-Man stuck with me well into my twenties. I can remember hundreds of times curling my hand the way Peter Parker did in the movies and expecting spider webs to shoot out.

I even remember actively seeking spiders that were radioactive in hopes of the spider biting me and giving me a superpower. As you may have suspected, I am *not* a real life Spider-Man, and there's a good chance that it's never going to happen. I had come to terms with the possibility of never having super powers or an incredible talent handed to me, never having a compelling motivator, like avenging my uncle's death, or having a cute neighbor like Mary Jane to inspire me to be my best self.

There are some quotes in movies that are memorable, and the movie *Spider-Man* has one. Peter Parker's uncle, Ben, gives Peter some words of wisdom, "With great power, comes great responsibility." Do you agree with that quote? It makes sense to me. If you get bit by a radioactive spider and become Spider-Man, there should be some responsibility on your part to use your super powers to fight crime and take down villains.

If you have an IQ that makes you a genius, there should be some responsibility on your part to become a doctor and find a cure for cancer. If you have some extraordinary gift or talent, there is some responsibility on your part to use it wisely. But what if you're like Peter Parker *before* the spider bite? What if you're an ordinary person, living an ordinary life, having no outside force act on you to give you extraordinary powers that cause you to act now and act in big ways? You're powerless.

I felt powerless working at a pharmacy years ago. I had been working there for four years and was making $9 an hour. My evaluation had come up with my boss, Frank, an Italian guy from New Jersey who's passionate about cooking and the New York Mets, and I was hoping for a raise. I believed I deserved it because I was never late, and had often come in when the pharmacy was short-staffed.

"Frank, I've been here for four years and I feel I should be making more than $9 per hour. I'm not asking for much, just an extra quarter an hour." I exclaimed. "I'm sorry, Mike. I can't give you a 25-cent raise, my supervisor won't allow me to do so."

I was disappointed and whined to my mom about it, but eventually let it go. After all, I had no power to change my fate. Then the following week I overheard Frank talking to another coworker of mine, Rachel, a girl my age who resembled Cameron Diaz. What my boss said to her made me furious and want to quit.

It was a few minutes before 9 a.m., when the pharmacy opens, and I heard Frank say, "Rachel, a 50 cent per hour raise is the most I could give you on this form, but I made a special request with my supervisor to give you a dollar extra per hour and he agreed. You're now going to be making $13.25 per hour."

She makes $13.25!? That's not fair! How on earth is she making $4.25 more than me and I've been working here 3 years longer than her? Frank lied to me. He said he couldn't give me a quarter raise, yet for her he finds a way to give her a dollar extra more per hour.

The only thing that made sense to me is that she was a pretty girl, a power an average looking guy like myself could not use. I wanted to talk to my boss about why he lied to me, but I was never one for confrontation. I preferred to whine and complain (mostly to my mom) about how unfair life was. I couldn't wait to get home after my shift that night and vent to momma.

"Mom, can you believe this? $4.25 cents more per hour with three years less experience, it would be nice if life was fair and people got paid for the quality of their work, and not based on their attractiveness."

When you vent to a loved one, you expect them to have your back. I was surprised by her response, "Michael, is it possible that her looks have nothing to do with it, and that she's a better worker than you?"

I was so thrown off by that question and it took me 15 seconds to process it before I could answer truthfully, "Yes, mom. It's possible." That's when it hit me, that my boss wasn't lying to me. He couldn't give me a raise, because I didn't deserve it. He was able to give Rachel a raise, because she did.

She was delightful to be around. She had an upbeat, positive attitude, always had a smile, and was incredible with people. She was metaphorical sunshine. She also worked twice as hard as me. I started to see why she deserved to make what she made, and I knew it had nothing to do with her looking like Cameron Diaz.

That may have been the first time I took responsibility for what was happening in my life. I realized I made $9 an hour because that's what I deserved. I had a negative attitude and brought other people down; I wasn't a people person and was not good with customers; and I was not working as hard as I knew I could have. I was a metaphorical dark cloud.

Letting go of excuses and blaming others put responsibility on me. Once I did this I finally felt hopeful that my life could change. With it being on me, I knew I could make changes, and knowing I had a say in my fate made me feel powerful.

I thought about that quote said to Peter Parker and started to believe the reverse was true. Maybe, if you are not where you'd like to be in your life and feel powerless, then "With great power, comes great responsibility" doesn't apply to you. However, what if you were to reverse Uncle Ben's quote and instead believe "With great responsibility, comes great power"?

You see, I was powerless when I believed I didn't get the raise because I didn't look like Cameron Diaz. However, when I believed the truth, that I was a dark cloud with my negative attitude, that I had poor people skills, and I had an average worth ethic, I started to be responsible. It made me uncomfortable accepting this, but once I did, I was able to take control of changing my actions, which led to me having more power in my life.

I stopped being bitter towards Rachel and started striving to become more like her. I focused more on having a better attitude, learning from my mistakes, and smiling more, even though it was hard work at first. It appeared people actually liked me after I made these changes. It's amazing what taking responsibility can do for you. It gives you the power to change your life. I started getting above and beyond the raises I wanted and didn't have to look like Cameron Diaz to do it!

It made me nauseous knowing I wasted years of my life choosing to make myself powerless by making a bunch of excuses and blaming others so that I could *feel* better. I could have just taken responsibility for my life and *became* better. I'm not saying taking responsibility for your life will be fun, but if you're lacking power, it's one of the best ways to gain it.

It was tough accepting that I didn't deserve a raise because I was not a good worker. It was tough accepting I didn't have many friends because I was not making the effort to *be* a friend. It was tough accepting that a majority of people in my life were more successful than me not because of luck, but because they earned it.

I almost wanted to not accept the truth and blame things outside of my control, to stay a victim and seek sympathy from my mom, but mamma stopped giving it to me. I almost wanted to keep blaming life for being unfair while remaining stuck where I am. Have you ever done what I did with that pharmacy job I had in college? Instead of believing that your co-worker deserved the promotion or raise, or believing your friend deserved their big break, do you believe they got lucky? Or do you believe it was because of their looks, connections, or some power they have that you don't?

Without question doing this can make you feel better for not being where you'd like to be in life. But it can make you feel powerless. I love the Spider-Man movies and love Uncles Ben's "With great power, comes great responsibility" quote. However, if you're feeling powerless you'll love reversing the quote and applying it to your life even more.

"With great responsibility, comes great power."

CHAPTER 5

THE OTHER SIDE OF THE FENCE

If you're looking for life to teach you something, be ready to take notes. Ever since I've been looking for the other side of life, several wise people have come to teach me. Ron is one of them.

Ron is in his late-30s, and a successful software salesman who's wise beyond his years. He's given me wisdom that I'll be sharing with others for decades.

However, there was one Sunday night when we were out walking and it was my turn to share some wisdom with him. We were in his neighborhood walking near the basketball court when he shouted, "Why would someone do that!?" I had no idea what he was talking about. He then pointed to the fence around the basketball court. It must have been about 20 feet high. He said, "Why would someone climb that? It could kill them!"

It *did* look like someone climbed it. It was bent at the top and sagging. I agreed with Ron; climbing that unusually high fence could have killed someone. I even looked at the court just to make sure there weren't any blood stains from someone's fall. There weren't.

I paused for a moment to think about why someone would take such a big risk to play on the basketball court. Then a thought came to me that was too good to keep to myself. "Ron, I know why this kid climbed the fence. He's a big dreamer. He probably wants to be the next Michael Jordan or Lebron James and doesn't have a basketball court in his neighborhood. So, what he does, is he comes here to work on his game, so that he can develop his greatness."

I was becoming giddy over this inspirational story in the making. I pictured ten years later this kid, let's call him Charles Cameron, is now a full-grown NBA star on ESPN being interviewed after winning a championship. The interviewer asks, "Charles, what made you so great?" "Man, it was dedication. I was dedicated to working on my game every day. In fact, I would even ride my bike over to the neighborhood court that had an unusually high fence. I thought scaling it would end badly every time, but I climbed it hundreds of times and got my hours of practice in. The key to my success was dedication."

I drifted off for fifteen seconds and played that scenario in my head before Ron responded to me. "No, Michael, that doesn't make sense. I still don't understand why someone would climb that fence."

All I was thinking was, *Ron's not a dreamer. That's why he doesn't understand. I'm a dreamer and it makes perfect sense to me.* Then he said, "I don't know why someone would climb the fence when the gate is open on the other side. The gate is *always* open." And my inspirational story became a silly one.

On the other side of the court, the gate was wide open. Our potential basketball star, Charles Cameron, wouldn't have had to climb the fence, he wouldn't have had to risk his life. All he had to do was walk through the open gate.

This story is a powerful metaphor for life. Maybe you don't want to be the next NBA star, but you do want to be or do something. You want to achieve that thing because of the feeling it will give you; maybe it's peace, security, confidence, a feeling of self-worth.

You can get there by climbing, *or* you can go to the other side and *walk right through*. Charles Cameron, our made up NBA star who climbed the fence to victory, was in such a rush to work on his goal that he didn't take the time to scan his surroundings. If he took the time to look around, he would have seen the easier, and more practical, option.

Just like in your life, taking a moment to pause, possibly seeking advice from the wise, can give you solutions that make you feel as if you're walking through the gate as opposed to climbing a fence that could kill you. There are several ways the metaphor can play out in your life, but the one that speaks to me loudest of all is your self-worth.

When you feel like you don't play a valuable role in life, it's easy to feel like you're on the outside looking in, watching other people play on the court of life. You can feel like there's a twenty foot fence blocking you from playing your own part. During these times, it's easy to have low self-esteem, to believe that you're not enough.

You can approach your fence in the following two ways.

The first is choosing to believe that you can't play a part in life and you can never be enough. Since you believe there's no hope, you never climb the fence. You don't risk hurting yourself since you never climb, but since you never climb you remain a spectator in life. Being a spectator will likely lead to you becoming bitter and jealous of others who are playing a role on the court. This option, which many take, leads to a lot of regret and an empty life.

Several others approach the fence with the second way. They think they are not enough *right now*, but they can be enough *someday* if they work on it. Maybe it's improving their physical appearance through diet and exercise. Maybe it's gaining higher status by raising their income or driving a nicer car, having a bigger house, or gaining more followers on Instagram.

The hope of being enough someday is there, so the desire to climb is there, too. But this constant climb is draining. Plus the higher up they go, the greater the chance they will experience a fall that they can't survive. Hustling to earn your self-worth and believing you have to climb to be enough is another way of missing out on a fulfilling life.

At various times in my life I took one of these two choices. At times, I was depressed because I believed I could *never* make it on the court and play a role in life. Other times, I believed if I looked better, had more money, or was more popular a role would be handed to me *someday*. Then I was reminded of a double date in high school I had with a good friend, Alex.

There's no denying Alex is a handsome guy. Blue eyes, chiseled jaw, and sculpted like a Greek God. Maybe I was jealous of him a tad, but he had been a great wingman for me. Alex was able to convince a girl he met through MySpace to bring one of her friends so the four of us could go on a double date. Our plans were to meet the girls somewhere fancy, like our local Applebee's. After that, we'd see where the magical night would take us. We were taking Alex's car, since it was deemed cooler than my green, '95 Mercury Sable.

I pulled up to Alex's house and walked inside. I was nervous about everything at that point in my life, but that night I was confident and excited. I had on a burgundy Abercrombie polo that fit me perfectly; the sleeves were really tight, constricting my arms and making me look more muscular than I really was. Plus, I was grateful to have a pretty girl go out with me and just as pumped over the dinner at Applebee's. In terms of rating on physical attractiveness one to ten, you'd likely say Alex is a 10 out of 10, and at the very least, the better-looking guy between the two of us.

However, it was Alex who was nervous and anxious about the date. I had a hard time processing why he was getting so worked up. "Alex, what are you nervous about? All the girls in school fawn all over you. I'm kind of jealous of you, to be honest." He pointed to the left side of his upper cheek. There was a little red bump I had to look hard for to even notice. "It's this pimple, Mike." "Alex, you're a 10 even with the pimple. Relax. I'm the one who should be freaking out about this date, not you."

I will never forget his response. "Mike, with this pimple, I'm *only* a 9.5." I thought, *you've got to be kidding me! Only* a 9.5? *I have no sympathy for you.* I couldn't believe my physical specimen of a friend was so insecure that he wanted to cancel our date. As years have passed I can empathize with Alex "only being a 9.5". You see, I thought my friend was plenty worthy and I'm sure his date felt the same way. But *he* didn't. It didn't matter what others thought; he wasn't good enough *in his own eyes.* He believed he wasn't worthy until he felt like a 10. He was holding himself back.

I now realize being a "5" and feeling like you're enough is better than being a "9.5" and believing you need to be a 10. Making $30,000 a year and feeling enough is better than making 10 million dollars a year and believing you need to make 20 million. This sense of worth is not something you get from others, it's what you give yourself.

Author Bren'e Brown helped me take something valuable from this double date story, to help you avoid falling into the same trap my friend Alex was in. In the book *Daring Greatly*, she discusses ten guideposts to "Wholehearted living." People living wholeheartedly are definitely living life to the fullest.

Bren'e Brown says the wholehearted have this is common, a sense of worthiness. They believe they are worthy and know they are enough. These types of people don't climb fences to get inside the court, they simply walk to the other side and walk through the open gate. Please don't misinterpret what I'm saying here.

I'm not saying that just because you believe you're worthy of being a NBA superstar means you're going to be offered a multi-million dollar contract to play on the Los Angeles Lakers. As our fictional basketball star, Charles Cameron, said in his fake ESPN interview, dedication is the key to success.

Charles might not be the best person to listen to. He was climbing that 20 foot fence and neglected to see that he could have been walking through the open gate. There is tremendous power in removing those fences, though. Imagine having a dream to play a part in making a positive difference in this world and you knew it was possible. It wasn't about making millions of dollars or being famous, but being skilled in something, being able to contribute to others in a unique way.

Because you knew that you had value, you would always be able to be on a court. Because you knew you had value, you would never have to climb. Instead you could devote all your energy to sharpening your skills on the court, as opposed to having to climb to make it on the court. Again, since your self-worth is no longer in question, you can be humble and let others teach you, advise you, and support you.

You would no longer have this intense desire to be in the spotlight, or be the star player. You would simply be on the court, grateful for your role, and trying to excel at it in the greatest way possible. I hope this metaphor changes your life the way it has mine. You see, I *love* what I'm doing right now, looking for life lessons to share with you, but for a long time I wasn't doing what I love because of the twenty foot fence in my mind.

I thought, *No one would ever read this, no one would ever care what I have to say. There's no point of even trying to climb over this fence.* I also thought, *Maybe I can figure out social media, build a large following so people will see me as valuable and maybe after that I can play a positive role in their life. Maybe I can become better looking, maybe I could get another degree, maybe I could become a millionaire. Maybe then someone would value what I have to say.*

But that climb has been draining over the years as my focus has been raising my self-worth as opposed to doing what truly mattered to me: working on my writing and speaking skills in hopes of changing someone's life the way the late motivational speaker Zig Ziglar changed mine. I'm just being honest with you. Can you at least be honest with yourself? Is there a fence up in your life right now? Do you believe you're not enough and your self-worth is in question?

If there is a fence, have you become hopeless and are choosing to escape from life though pleasures such as tv, eating junk food, and whatever else takes your mind off your fence? Or are you trying to climb your fence? Are you trying to look better, have more material possessions, or more status? Maybe you're scaling up the fence, but how do you feel internally? Maybe others see you as scoring a 100 on the test of life, but they can't see the other side of you, the side that is making you feel like you're scoring a 50 because your self-worth is *constantly* in question.

I know it seems too good to be true, but there is another side to this fence. A side with an open gate, one you can easily walk through. Allow yourself to walk through it. Once you do, you'll start developing in ways you never imagined. As an example, I'm not tying my self-worth to how many people read this book. I'm simply sharing life lessons that radically changed my life. I hope they have the same effect on you.

That's it. I've walked through the open gate and I'm writing a chapter for this book. Every time I walk through the gate and write, I develop my writing skills. Every time I share my writing, it increases the chances of adding value to someone's life. It's incredibly fulfilling knowing those possibilities exist. However, it came *after* going to the other side and walking through the gate to get on the court.

Why someone would climb the fence when the gate is open on the other side? One that's *always* open? It's because they can only see two options that most take. You may have spent your entire life believing that being a spectator or climbing the fence were your only two options.

You have a third option. If you're not dreaming, or not pursuing a dream, it's likely because you're not seeing the third option when it comes to your self-worth. It's the open gate on the other side. It has been and *always* will be open. I believe you were destined to read this. You have a role to play on the court of life. Walk through the open gate, get on the court, and develop your greatness!

CHAPTER 6

EMBRACING YOUR SNOW

Syracuse, New York, is one of the snowiest cities in America. Snow brings freezing temperatures, which prevent people from working at their best. People also panic. Just the news of an impending snowstorm is enough to heighten the risk of someone getting stepped on as they go into the local Walmart to get teriyaki beef jerky and other essentials for the snowstorm. Snow throws off routines. Schools and businesses close and everyone is left playing catch up once they can open again. Lastly, snow is dangerous and can cause many car accidents.

A lot of people in Syracuse would be happier if it didn't snow as much, or better yet, stopped snowing all together. This is likely what the city's Common Council thought. In 1992, the Council passed a decree that any more snow before Christmas was illegal.

As it turns out, just because you make something illegal doesn't mean it won't happen. You can probably guess what happened two days after the decree was passed. It snowed. This decree was real, but it was more of a joke than a law they actually believed would solve the city's snow problem.

This story is silly, but we often try to outlaw mental and emotional "snow" in our lives. This snow represents the people and problems in our lives that make life more difficult.

I think of Michael Scott from *The Office*. In an episode in the fourth season titled "Money," Michael's finances are out of control. He's spending much more than he's bringing in. His debt is snowballing, but he comes up with a genius solution. He yells at the top of his lungs, "I declare bankruptcy!" He then feels relieved. He believes this allows him to avoid his snow. But then his co-worker, Oscar, explains to Michael that's not how bankruptcy works. Michael goes back to being devastated. How is it that we can laugh at Michael Scott for yelling "I declare bankruptcy!" but don't laugh when we are doing the same thing?

We might try to address our mental and emotional snow by declaring, "No more negative people!", "No more toxic people!", "No more stress!", "No more challenges!". But I'm sure you've realized, outlawing your snow is ineffective and downright silly.

Since we can't outlaw it, we may try to avoid it by going to a sunny climate. Apparently, it has never snowed in Key West, Florida. The lowest temperature it's ever seen was 41 degrees Fahrenheit; nine degrees above the freezing point necessary for snow.

Think about this: if everyone is avoiding their mental and emotional snow to go to a proverbial Key West, the traffic to get there would be horrendous, plus it would be so overpopulated that you would feel like you're at a Taylor Swift concert, except there's no music.

Plus, not having any problems in life may be the biggest problem of all. You'd never get the chance to grow as a person, and you couldn't develop your character. What if instead of outlawing or avoiding your mental and emotional snow, you instead *embraced* it?

Let's look at cold and cruel people. Can you think of anyone in your life who is like the grinch? They're hostile, mean, and their heart appears to be two sizes too small. Ron Howard's adaptation of Dr. Seuss' classic story of *How the Grinch Stole Christmas* provides a blueprint on how to handle the grinches in your life. Most of us treat real-life grinches the way the average Whoville town member did. They simply hate him, assume there's nothing good about him, and want nothing to do with him.

Having the curiosity of six-year-old Cindy Lou Who is a great place to start. She heard all these awful things about the Grinch, but that drove her to want to find out more about him. We can do the same. To at least entertain the possibility that negative conditions were present in their past to cause them to act the way they do now. As influential psychologist Albert Bandura has said and proven in his experiments, "Given appropriate social conditions, decent, ordinary people can be led to do extraordinarily cruel things."

Cindy Lou finds out that when the grinch was eight, he had a crush on Martha May. That year he got in the Christmas spirit like never before. He put a tremendous amount of work making an angel ornament for Martha to win her heart. But, he was letting what one of his classmates said the day before rattle him. Augustus Maywho, the bully who later became the mayor of Whoville, was also trying to win Martha's heart. Augustus told the eight-year-old grinch, "You don't have a chance with her. You're eight years old and you have a beard." The grinch became self-conscience, and decided to shave. He nicked his face badly, leaving him with dozens of pieces of tissue to blot his cuts. The Grinch is ashamed and puts a bag over his head. Augustus provides the class a reason for why he has the bag over his head, "It's probably because of that hideodorous gift!" The teacher pleads with the young grinch to remove the bag. It comes off and Augustus weighs in again, "Look at that hack job!" The whole class erupts with laughter, even the teacher. The grinch's shame turns into rage as he destroys the classroom and the ornament for Martha May and screams, "I hate Christmas!" He then leaves Whoville to go to Mount Crumpit, the town's garbage receptacle at the top of the mountain.

After learning this, Cindy Lou has compassion for the Grinch. She now believes that he was kind-hearted; he just let a humiliating event shrink his heart. Cindy Lou desires to get the Grinch to come down to Whoville by nominating him as Whoville's holiday Cheermeister. The town is baffled by her nomination since the Cheermeister is responsible for raising the Christmas spirit of the town, something the grinch completely lacks. The Mayor reluctantly agrees that the Grinch can be the holiday Cheermeister if Cindy Lou can get the grinch to attend.

Cindy used her curiosity to get a clearer picture of the grinch. Now she had to be persuasive.

There's something powerful that emerges when you're persuasive out of love and kindness towards another person. Cindy Lou points out that if the grinch is to attend he will make his nemesis, Mayor Augustus, upset; he will be able to showcase himself as a winner in front of his childhood crush, Martha May; and he will get a reward for being the Cheermeister. Cindy Lou leaves and the Grinch ponders out loud whether or not he should accept the offer.

"Even if I wanted to go, my schedule wouldn't allow it! 4 o'clock: wallow in self-pity. 4:30: stare into the abyss. **5 o'clock: solve world hunger (tell no one)**. 5:30: jazzercise. 6:30: dinner with me, I can't cancel that again! 7 o'clock: wrestle with my self-loathing. I'm booked! Course if I bump the loathing to 9 I can still be done in time to lay in bed, stare at the ceiling, and slip slowly into madness."

If your daily itinerary looked like this wouldn't you be bitter, mean, and have a heart that was two sizes too small also? I personally have never attended a jazzercise class, but I imagine it's amazing! But loneliness, self-loathing, and slipping slowly into madness can't possibly make you cheerful. You don't know what your real life grinch is going through, so it's best to start on the right foot, by approaching him or her with more empathy.

I highlighted what was on his 5 o'clock itinerary because adopting this belief will help you be more patient and compassionate towards your real life-grinch. **"Solve world hunger (tell no one)."** Choose to believe that deep down, everyone is kind-hearted and wants to add greater good to the world. Grinches want to do something noble like solving world hunger, but hide it because it's out of alignment with how they see themselves.

The grinch agreed to come down to Whoville to be its Cheermeister. The grinch was charming with all the Whos and it seems the story will have a happy ending. Then the Mayor offers the Grinch his award: a razor. The same type of razor the Grinch used to shave his face when he was eight. The grinch relives his humiliating childhood moment and the Whos are laughing at him. He seeks revenge by trying to steal Christmas.

He appears to succeed, taking all the presents, ornaments, and even the last can of Who-Hash. He believes the Whos will wake up sad on Christmas morning.

He's mistaken. When people realize you have joy inside you that can't be stolen, it can cause them to change their ways. While reflecting over his failed revenge attempt, Cindy Lou visits the grinch, and he wonders why. Her response causes the ice to melt off his heart, "I came to see you. No one should be alone on Christmas." It was Cindy Lou's undeserved kindness that changed his heart and changed his ways.

There's a proverb that states, "If your enemy is hungry, give him bread to eat, and if he is thirsty, give him water to drink, for you will heap burning coals on his head..." -Proverbs 25:21-22 ESV

Cindy Lou's kindness served as heaping, burning coals on the grinch's mind and heart. It caused him to think, *Why is this little girl being so kind to me? Maybe Cindy Lou sees my kind-hearted side, the side that wants to end world hunger and love others. Maybe it's time to show this side I've been hiding because of my pain.* We generally treat people how we see them. When Cindy Lou treated the Grinch kindly, he changed how he saw himself. As he saw himself different, he changed his ways. Cindy Lou is the hero of the story and is someone that should inspire us to be more compassionate to our real-life grinches.

We often wait for our real-life grinches to come down from their mountain of misery to where we are. We wait for them to apologize and make up for the wrongs they've done before considering being kind to them. Cindy Lou met the Grinch where he was, up on Mount Crumpit, the place of the town's trash, his place of misery, and brought kindness to where he currently was.

Real-life grinches need kindness the most, yet seldom receive it because we aren't approaching them like Cindy Lou. We don't investigate. We let others' opinions of them, or one isolated incident, define their entire identity. We don't give the person who cut us off in traffic the benefit of the doubt; we just assume they're a terrible person. We also assume our grinches been bitter and cruel their whole life and don't entertain the possibility that something has happened to them to behave this way. Plus, we often don't practice kindness towards someone until we believe they deserve it.

Are you currently experiencing emotional freezing temperatures in your life due to cold, real-life grinches? You might be waiting for *them* to change, but could it be *you* who needs to warm up by showing them kindness and compassion? If you're waiting for your grinches to change, you will likely be waiting for the rest of your life. However, if you approach your grinches like Cindy Lou did, your kindness will strengthen your character. Plus, there's a tremendous chance your kindness will melt the ice off their heart and cause their heart to grow bigger than ever before.

Maybe it's not *people* causing you to experience cold times in your life, but *moments.* Maybe your heart has been broken, you have a job that you loathe, or feel you're the unluckiest person in the world.

During these snowy moments think of this quote from Malcolm Forbes, "When things are bad, we take comfort in the thought that they could always get worse. And when they are, we find hope in the thought that things are so bad they have to get better."

Maybe during your tough time you're mentally and emotionally shivering and feel as if it's -30 degrees Fahrenheit. It's ice cold right now, but could be much worse. In 1983, a Russian research station in Antarctica, Vostok Station, recorded temperatures of -128.6 degrees Fahrenheit. *Negative 128.6!* Knowing that it could get worse can cause you to be grateful, to start seeing things that could warm you up. It could be having your family and friends there to support you as you find your way in life. You could have *nobody*.

However, when you're in your cold seasons, being told "be grateful" isn't what you want to hear. You may believe it really is the worst it's ever been and can't get any worse. This is the time to be hopeful. This is the time to realize how strong you are. If you honestly believe your proverbial temperature is -128.6 degrees then life can only heat up from this point on! You've held on and survived this long when it comes to your life and your goals. Why let go at the moment it's going to heat up?

Your low moments are where you find the most insights. As super bowl winning quarterback, John Elway, stated, "You learn a lot more from the lows because it makes you pay attention to what you're doing." Everyone experiences low moments. The key is getting the most out of them.

You can use your mental and emotional snow and ice in your low moments to build a mental igloo. The snow and ice acts like an insulator. It traps the body heat of those inside the igloo and keeps them warm. Did you know that if an igloo is built properly, the temperature outside can be -50 degrees, but your body can keep the inside heated to 60 degrees?

If the temperature is frigid for you right now, build a mental igloo. Slow down and pay more attention to what you're doing, and you'll have your igloo in seconds. Some questions to ask could be, "What can I learn from this?" and "What's the most important thing I can be doing right now?" Or it could be the time to recite something like the *Serenity Prayer*: "God, grant me the serenity to accept the things I cannot change, courage to change the things I can, and wisdom to know the difference."

Every time you ask a thought-provoking question such as those mentioned above, it's as if you're in a mental igloo. You're now using your creative brain power to come up with solutions that will likely heat up your freezing situation.

Snow and ice can also impair your vision. Think of ice on the windshield. The best thing to do would be to go out 30 minutes before you have to leave, turn the heat on, and let your car defrost. The only problem is that these mental and emotional times can occur unexpectedly. Without thawing, you could be traveling to your destination blind, going much slower and likely crashing. What if you were to pretend as if your vision was icy every morning and spent 30 minutes defrosting? These 30 minutes could be spent meditating, praying, reading inspirational material, or whatever else warms you up. This time thaws you out and lets you see life more clearly. This time also arms you with the thoughts necessary to build your mental igloos throughout your day.

However, the mental and emotional snow in your life presents itself, don't outlaw it like Syracuse did. That won't work. Embrace your snow. Embrace your grinches and have the heart to approach them like Cindy Lou did. Embrace those frigid temperatures, because with a thought-provoking quote or question you can build yourself a mental igloo to heat yourself up. And with your vision, thaw your ice by making a daily habit of at least 30 minutes of defrosting time. Collectively, all these ideas will warm you up during your snowy seasons and help you embrace your snow.

CHAPTER 7

WHERE THERE'S SMOKE...

Finish the sentence. Where there's smoke, there's....... what? If you answered "fire" that was the answer I was looking for, but by the time this chapter is over, you'll be answering it differently.

For the past year, the smoke alarm in my bedroom has been chirping constantly. Several times a day it would make the "Eh, eh, eh," sound, and I would just push the button to hush it. The smart thing to do would have been to investigate it further as soon as it started. *Maybe the detector is defective and needs a new one? Maybe I need to put a new nine volt battery in it?* Now, I'm kind of hoping the smoke detector magically fixes itself. All I do know is that out of the hundreds of times my smoke detector has chirped over the years, not *once* has there been a fire.

One day, I thought, *The chirping is so annoying! Plus, what are the odds of a fire actually happening? This detector is a nuisance. I'm taking the battery out to end this madness.* So, I took the battery out of the smoke detector in my bedroom, but that didn't solve my problem. It still chirped! Several times it would wake me up in the middle of the night and I had reached my breaking point. *Once again, what are the odds of a fire actually happening?* I believed the odds were slim, and reached for that smoke detector and was about to yank it off the ceiling like I was starting a lawn mower.

As I was about to do this, I could hear my mom's voice in my head, "Michael, sweetie, don't do that. If your house has a fire, you'll need that. Please keep that detector, and fix it." I let out a deep sigh to my mom's imaginary comment, knew that she was right, and let go of the smoke detector. Fire is a strange thing. At times we do everything we can to acquire it, such as when we are stranded on an island like Tom Hanks in *Castaway*. In this case, fire would save your life. It would keep you warm and heat up the raw fish you caught. Then there's my scenario, where I have all my trinkets and knick knacks around my house. A fire could burn my house down, leaving me without the aforementioned trinkets and knick knacks, making life dreadfully inconvenient.

Let's look at your dream as starting a fire. Your dream is the fire you want, like the fire from our *Castaway* example, not the fire that melts your trinkets and knick knacks. Whatever your dream is, you actually living it would represent a blazing fire. First off, what is your dream? I find most people have an enormous dream that they are often scared to share with anyone, and one that is less ambitious and more practical. Does this ring true for you? Take a moment and give this some thought.

The reason we usually don't pursue, or even share the enormous dreams, is because the gap between that dream and reality is so large it's comical.

It's as if your dream is a blazing fire big enough to host a bonfire party for your 10-year high school reunion, but your reality is just a smidgeon of smoke.

I'm learning that if you want to stay persistent in building the blazing fire in your current reality, you shouldn't get discouraged when there's no fire. You should get *encouraged* when you see smoke, and then build on it. The smoke in your dream are reasons to be hopeful and signs of progress towards the fire. If you have hope in your dream being fulfilled, your dream detector chirps from time to time.

But just like my bedroom smoke detector, it's often a false alarm. The kitchen smoke detector could go off because you're cooking pasta and you let it steam too much. Or maybe it's because you need to replace the battery. Whatever the false alarm is, if it happens too much, you become like I was with my smoke detector in my bedroom, and you consider yanking the battery out to hush it.

But once again, in this metaphor, smoke is good! We want all smoke detected, because if we detect it, we can build on it, add wood to it, and eventually have the blazing fire. Even if false alarms occur, we can't risk missing out on that smidgeon of smoke that leads to our fire.

Sometimes your dream detector could be chirping for years, or even decades, before the blazing fire presents itself. I believe that's why people stop dreaming. There are too many false chirps. If you keep hoping for something and it never happens, it's disappointing, even heart breaking. To avoid this disappointment, many see the solution as ripping out their dream detector, the detector that goes off with hope, the detector that goes off with progress.

What's truly heartbreaking is someone who is so close to having that blazing fire come into their life, but walking away from it prematurely. They had the smoke and enough wood to build their fire, but they turned off their smoke detector because they could no longer bear being hopeful without tangible results. They were making progress, but the progress wasn't fast enough for them, so they gave up. It's tragic.

Are you focusing too much on your fire and not enough on your smoke? The "fire," the dream you want fulfilled, might not be here yet, and it isn't likely to come soon, at least if it's a big dream. However, if your dream detector is on, and is extremely sensitive to even a smidgen of smoke, you could choose to believe that every time it goes off it puts a smile on your face. This smoke is *any* reason to be hopeful, *any* sign of progress. You can choose to believe that you're closer to the blazing fire than you were before. For example, let's say you want to lose 50 pounds. You've dieted and exercised intensely for a week. You hop on the scale and see you've only lost one pound. One pound seems insignificant, but it's a smidgen of smoke. It's better than nothing. In fact, repeat this result fifty times and you will have reached your weight loss goal in under a year. Repeat zero pounds lost fifty times and you'll still find yourself at zero.

I haven't shared this with many people, but believe I've struggled with some case of Obsessive Compulsive Disorder. I was never officially diagnosed or saw a doctor, but I had an obsession with the number ten. I believed I had to do certain things ten times. I'd check to make sure my door was locked ten times so no one would break in. I'd check my wallet ten times to make sure I had my money and credit cards. I'd sometimes read my notes ten times when studying. I'd brush my eyebrows ten times and tap my pencil on my desk ten times in college before tests, thinking that it would help me ace it.

It's completely irrational, but I did it for several years. I thought it kept me safe and gave me luck. A few years ago I got over my obsession with ten by strengthening my faith and realizing I have more control over my thoughts than I realized. I share this with you because I've made a friend recently, Luke, who is struggling with OCD. He reached out to me for advice after I shared some of this personal information with him. I'm realizing if you share your struggles with others, it's likely there is someone out there who you can help with the same struggle and connect with them in a way most people can't.

Talking with Luke, I could sense the hopelessness in his voice. He told me he spent up to four hours of his day checking his locks and windows, and spent a long time analyzing his food for fear someone was trying to harm him. He also was a bit of a recluse, not socializing with anyone outside of his parents.

Luke's issue was that he was wanting to be completely OCD-free from day one. He wanted a blazing fire right away. I wanted him to generate hope that he wasn't stuck where he was. I wanted him to make daily progress. I wanted him to focus on finding smoke and building on it. For about a month we were talking on a daily basis and I would ask, "What was your smoke for the day?" The first time, he said he spent five less minutes checking his locks and windows. He knew this because I asked him to time himself whenever he was performing his rituals. As far as interacting with people, I was looking for any progress, even waving at a kid riding on his bicycle. Over the next couple weeks, each and every day he would have some "smoke" to share with me. Whether it be shaving off minutes from performing his rituals, having casual conversations with his neighbors, to even just recently when he told me he was going to visit family members for the holidays, something he never saw himself doing.

As time went on, Luke's tone changed. He was hopeful. He knew he was making progress. I told him the story about my bedroom smoke detector and even made the annoying "eh, eh, eh!" noise after he shared his progress. I'm incredibly grateful to witness someone overcome "Popeye Syndrome." It's not a real syndrome. You won't find it on WebMD. It's something I made up, inspired by Popeye the Sailor Man. I'm sure you remember him for eating spinach to gain his strength, but I remember him saying, "I am what I am, and that's all that I am." People with "Popeye Syndrome" believe they're stuck where they are and can never change.

You see, Luke had wanted a blazing fire, to be completely free from his rituals and social anxiety due to his OCD, but every day he observed his current reality and saw no fire. Years of the giant gap from dreams and reality caused him to lose hope and feel stuck. With limited hope, he lost his drive to overcome his struggles.

Then Luke shifted his approach. He wanted a blazing fire, but his focus was now on smoke. This smoke, again, were the reasons to be hopeful, the signs of progress. The hope and the progress help him realize his blazing fire is possible. He just needs to be on the lookout for a smidgen of smoke, and once he detects it, work on building from it.

I can tell he's more alive and hopeful than ever, because he has weeks of waking up every day having his internal smoke detector going off, and building on it. He's a kind-hearted young man and I'm eager to see what he does with his life, but for now, let's use this metaphor in *your* life.

Are you making the same mistake Luke, and almost everyone I know including myself, is making? Are you wanting to be free from that struggle or bad habit *right now*, to be working your dream job *right now*, to have anything that represents a blazing fire *right now*, and devastated that you currently don't see the blazing fire? Maybe you're convinced it's impossible. Unfortunately, having that blazing fire *right now* is likely impossible. However, smoke that makes you hopeful, the smoke that indicates progress, is likely already present in your life. Are you failing to focus on the smoke because you're looking for fire? Have you turned off your internal smoke detector because of too many false alarms? Are you struggling with Popeye Syndrome? Do you wake up and talk to yourself in the mirror and say, "I am what I am, and that's I that I am?"

To use a simple example, I've read that up to 81 percent of Americans say that they would like to write a book someday. I attended a Christmas party recently where a majority had "writing a book" as one of their lifelong aspirations. Why aren't you writing that book you want? Probably the same reason this book took years to write. I was focused on the blazing fire. I fantasized having the book done and handing a copy to all the people who have helped and supported me throughout my life. When I'd wake up and not even have the book started, the blazing fire seemed to be something

I could only see in my imagination. Then I turned on my internal smoke detector and started scanning for smoke. Largely due to the fact that this was the advice I gave my friend Luke, and didn't want to be a hypocrite.

I found that I was getting the same results Luke was. Each sentence I typed out was a smidgeon of smoke. Here's another smidgeon with this sentence. Here's some more. Wow, look at this, I have a paragraph of smoke that was not present fifteen seconds ago! Smoke detectors can alert you of good and bad news. Both are better than being uninformed of any smoke at all.

Let's look at writing. Everything you write is smoke, but it's not the "same" kind of smoke. Some things you write will be "good smoke". It's entertaining and insightful. Building off of this smoke is valuable and can lead to a great story, the blazing fire you want.

But there's also another type of smoke that seems bad. Maybe what you wrote is boring or confuses everyone. Without my editor, who is my book's smoke detector, my book would be full of this "bad smoke". But even having your detector on for this "bad smoke" is still good, because it lets you know of the necessary changes needed to make the "good smoke" that leads to progress.

My friend, I hope that you have a dream, that it's a blazing fire, one that not only enriches your life, but causes you to enrich other lives, too. I truly hope I can share your success story someday, but I'm not sure I'll be able to if you don't have your internal smoke detector on. Again, for this metaphor, smoke of all kinds is good.

People tend to underestimate what smoke in a person's dream can do to them. They underestimate what hope can do; they also fail to realize what progress, even as small as writing a sentence towards their novel, can do. Hope motivates them to take action on whatever their fire represents, whether it be losing weight, quitting smoking, or getting a degree.

That action often leads to progress, and that progress generates hope. It's not a vicious cycle, but a virtuous one. A cycle that can take a hopeless person, one who believes they can never change their current situation or who they are, and fill them with so much hope for their future that they can't help but inspire other people.

Please keep your smoke detector on. Don't rip out your smoke detector because of the annoying chirp when there's no fire. Your smoke detector is in your house to save your life; your internal smoke detector is in your heart to save your dream. We started this chapter with "Where there's smoke, there's fire" and I want you to look at it in a different way. Where there's smoke, there's hope. Where there's smoke, there's progress. Where there's smoke, there's a blazing dream in the making. Where there's smoke, there's a chance to change for the better.

Be on the alert when you see smoke and don't let it die out. Build on it, keep looking for reasons to be hopeful. Keep looking for progress, no matter how small. You're not Popeye the Sailor Man and you don't have "Popeye Syndrome." Stop saying, "I am what I am and that's all that I am." You are *never* stuck where you are. The fire you kindle in your life will depend on your ability to build off your smoke. Focus on finding your daily smoke, and I'm positive you'll give yourself an amazing chance at having a blazing fire one day.

CHAPTER 8

SCALING MOUNT SUCCESS

If I gave you a five-step program on how you can scale the proverbial mountain, Mount Success, would you be interested? Mount Success is twice the height of Mount Everest, which is over 29,000 feet and only one in a million people have reached this level of success in life. Why so few? They don't know the five steps.

To sweeten the deal, what if I told you that if you followed them you could reach the peak of Mount Success by tomorrow? To make the deal even sweeter (as if that's even possible) the five step program can be yours with seven easy payments of $29.95. Wait, there's more! If you buy within the next hour I'll even knock off one of the seven easy payments. That's right! You could be on Mount Success by tomorrow in five easy steps and for only six easy payments of $29.95!

That was quite a compelling pitch, don't you think? Felt a little cheesy typing that out, but I want you to pretend that Mount Success is a real place. Pretend the five steps got you to the top, and not only did it get you to the top, it got you there by tomorrow.

But if I told you I wouldn't want to be at the top of Mount Success *by tomorrow* you'd think I was foolish. However, there's a part of the quick ascent up the mountain you may not be thinking of. Altitude sickness.

Altitude sickness is caused by reduced air pressure and lower oxygen levels at high altitudes. The faster you climb, the more likely you'll experience this sickness. According to the Cleveland Clinic, symptoms of altitude sickness include headaches, vomiting, weakness, tiredness, trouble sleeping, and lack of appetite. Severe cases, which would certainly occur when you scale a mountain twice the height of Mount Everest by tomorrow, include high altitude pulmonary edema (HAPE) with associated shortness of breath or high altitude cerebral edema (HACE) with associated confusion.

Basically HAPE is fluid in the lungs and HACE is fluid in the brain. These are the dangers of quick ascension up Mount Success. It's great you made it up there. I'm sure your mom is so proud of you, and you will have a great Instagram photo of you on top of Mount Success to share, but this book is much deeper than obtaining superficial success.

We make the mistake of trying to scale Mount Success as fast as possible, but we don't think about how to live at the top of Mount Success without experiencing altitude sickness. Think about all these symptoms of altitude sickness. You'll have a headache and be vomiting. You'll be tired, but you'll have trouble falling asleep. Plus, you won't have an appetite. My research is referring to a physical appetite, but on Mount Success, you won't have a mental or psychological appetite to achieve more, as well.

One symptom that stuck out to me was the high-altitude cerebral edema (fluid in the brain). If you were to scale Mount Success in a day, your head would swell so big, you would think you are the smartest person in the world. With a head this big, you wouldn't be receptive to learning from others, which almost guarantees you won't scale any higher in life.

I'm grateful to have many wise people teach me this lesson and I'm also grateful I was able to find a metaphor to make the lesson easier to grasp. I believe this concept was inspired by a mentor of mine who evaluated videos I sent him of me giving motivational speeches. He told me he watched twenty or thirty of them.

I asked him, "Well, what do you think? Do you think I have what it takes to be great someday?" His response was, "Right now I have no clue. I need to know what you're made of, I need to know if your character is strong enough that it's not shaken by the ups and downs of life."

I feel the same way about you, reader. I truly believe you're not on this earth simply to exist. You're here to contribute to the world in a unique way. The potential is there for *something*. It may not be as glamorous as being a supermodel, singer, or professional athlete, but the potential is there. You just need to think deeper. It's not only about reaching Mount Success quickly, it's about going as high as you can go while avoiding altitude sickness.

I said one in a million have reached Mount Success, but how many of them are experiencing altitude sickness and can hide it really well? Especially on social media. You can stand tall and flex on top of Mount Success while you take a selfie, then collapse as soon as you've uploaded your photo on Instagram with the following hashtags: #MountSuccess #Hustler #Determined #Fighter #Warrior #DontHateMeCauseYouAintMe. Okay, I'm getting carried away with the hashtags. I'll stop now. #micdrop. Okay, *now* I'm really done.

Maybe there is a five-step program out there that gets you to the top of Mount Success, but I'm certain that program won't develop your character to the point you can comfortably *live there*. Please believe me, I don't want what I'm saying to be true. I would love to take my decades of foolishness, mistakes, and insights and condense them into five steps that you could absorb in a day.

But as one of my mentors has told me, "Nothing speaks like experience." We can say how we would handle fame and success, but we won't know for sure until we experience it. For example, I remember a time in high school when a good friend and I went to a college basketball game. We somehow found a way to sneak into the locker room and found one of the star players who was a year away from being a top ten draft pick in the following year's NBA draft. We asked for his autograph and he snapped at us. "Ugh! I'm not signing autographs right now." I thought if I had someone asking for *my* autograph, I would be grateful and appreciative.

However, I don't know that for sure. Most of us don't know what that level of fame is like. I imagine being in this guy's shoes. Everywhere he goes, people want his autograph because he's highly skilled at basketball. He's not getting the attention for who he *is*, he's getting it for what he *does*. It can wear on him wondering how people would treat you him if he wasn't so skilled at basketball. It often takes time to understand that you're so much more than what you do. Understanding something like that doesn't occur overnight.

You can read all the relationship books in the world, but until you're actually in one you won't know how you'll handle it. Same with raising a child. Same with ascending up a mountain quickly. Maybe it's just me, but when I thought about climbing a mountain, altitude sickness didn't come to mind. But when I started researching climbing a mountain, not to actually climb one, but to write this chapter and make the concepts factual, I learned about altitude sickness.

There is even a rule of thumb when climbing a mountain: you shouldn't ascend more than 1,000 feet per day. You can't rush climbing a mountain, and this is why climbers need to spend days (even weeks at times) acclimatizing before attempting to scale a high peak. No one, I mean no one, wants to hear that the process cannot safely be rushed.

It takes wisdom and understanding to see past the cheesy salesman promising you a 58,000-foot ascension in one day. It takes wisdom and understanding to listen to the mountain climbing expert who has scaled the mountain multiple times while avoiding altitude sickness. But most of us don't have the patience to ascend only 1,000 feet per day. I certainly didn't. I remember earlier this year trying to find my purpose in life, so I read *The Purpose Driven Life* by Rick Warren.

The author recommended one chapter per day and to answer the reflection questions at the end of each chapter. Did I do that? Of course not. I went through it in four days and blew right by the discussion questions at the end of the chapter, because it was too much work, and took too much of my time. A few weeks later I ran into a friend and he asked me what I thought of the book. I told him, "It was really great. There was a lot of great material in it, but I still think I'm looking for my purpose."

I then revealed that I didn't follow the author's instructions and didn't answer the questions and my friend replied, "No wonder you didn't get anything out of it. I'm going to suggest you go through it one chapter at a time and seriously give some thought to all the reflection questions." I went through it again, this time, one chapter per day, and took the time to give deep thought to all the discussion questions. I got a lot more out of it the second time when I didn't rush the process.

Don't you see what happened? I was so eager to find my purpose and couldn't wait another second. So I thought I would stay up late each night reading until one in the morning, just like many of us are "hustling" to scale Mount Success as fast as possible. However, some of the ideas in the book took time for me to acclimate to them, and change me on the inside. Some of the ideas required me to sit still and process.

I do think the *Purpose Driven Life* by Rick Warren is an excellent book, but the concept I'm discussing in this chapter is much deeper than getting the most out of a book. It's about acclimating on the inside, so that when you reach high levels of success, you don't let that success swell your head, you don't lose the drive that got you there, and your motives and morals stay intact.

Again, please think deeper. You want to *attain* success, but you also want to *maintain* it too. Accept the fact that you're not going to reach the top of Mount Success by tomorrow and not experience altitude sickness. Do what I've been trying to do recently; wake up and focus on climbing *your* 1,000 feet. Forget about those around you who are climbing at a faster rate. Have the wisdom to know that the process of being a success inside and outside *cannot* be rushed.

There are some events in life that you'll have to simply experience to fully understand, and to fully develop your character. Ignore get-rich-quick schemes. Ignore anyone who gives you a bogus sales pitch like mine at the beginning of this chapter. Many people scale Mount Success, but those who do it the right way, without any altitude sickness, are even fewer. Be one of those who scales your mountain the right way.

Do you want to reach the highest peak in life safely without any symptoms of altitude sickness? It's going to take time. You're going to have to be patient. Don't fret over the time it will take, just focus on your 1,000 feet for today. What is your thousand-foot climb for the day? At the end of the day, reflect on how far you've traveled and if it is aligned with what you planned, and how it wasn't. Then find out what changes you need to make to keep making progress. Get in the habit of answering how you're going to scale your daily 1,000 feet and watch how much more you improve on the inside and out.

Absorb today's wisdom, today's life lessons, and take the time to reflect and *acclimate* while you elevate up Mount Success. #ChapterOver

CHAPTER 9

THE ANSWER IS YES. NOW, WHAT'S THE QUESTION?

Is there anyone in your life who you would say yes to before hearing what they ask of you? Maybe you think of your significant other, one of your kids, a brother or sister, or maybe a best friend of yours. It's rare that we commit to doing something for someone before knowing what it is.

The most likely time you'll be asked to commit without knowing what lies ahead is marriage. "I (insert your name here), take you, (Insert spouse name here, make it Taylor Swift or John Stamos if you want) to be my lawfully wedded (husband/wife), to have and to hold, from this day forward, for better, for worse, for richer, for poorer, in sickness and in health, until death do us part." "I do," the groom/bride exclaims.

But throughout our lives, people change, circumstances change, and so does our commitment. Not all marriages last. Not all of our emphatic yeses stay that way as life goes on.

There was only one time in my life I can recall where I was asked to commit before I knew what was being asked of me. It was my best friend, Ben. For many years he was my only friend. After school we had drifted apart, but his wedding brought us back together. We got to a point where we were almost talking on a daily basis. On September 21st, 2017, he called me and was asking me to give a yes without knowing the question. "Hey, Mike. What does your schedule look like this weekend?" "I've been working a ton over the past couple weeks, but have the next four days off." "Mike, that's great, because I'm about to ask something of you that's very important, and I need you to say yes to it."

"Ben, what's so important?" "Mike, I need you to promise me you'll do it before I tell you." I started to get nervous. *Did he murder someone and wants me to help him hide the body? Did he steal drugs from a drug lord and wants to hide them at my house?* We went back and forth a couple times, but he wouldn't budge. I needed to promise to say yes and commit before I knew what I had to do.

I paused a moment to think about all he had done for me. I remember the time I met him on the golfing range the day before the high school tryouts. I remember the way I was swinging the club. I had no chance of making the golf team, but he spent hours with me helping me fix my swing. With his help, I made the team.

I remember after one golf match, the team was at Hardee's and I didn't have any money. I was the only kid not eating, and I was sitting at a table by myself. He came over and gave me half of his burger. I'm not going to talk too much about our friendship and get teary-eyed about it. The point I'm trying to make is that he has always been there for me. I wanted to be there for him. "Okay, Ben. I promise. The answer is yes. Now what's the question?"

"Okay, Mike, this may sound crazy, but remember, you said yes to this, and you promised." He continued, "There is a planet called Nibiru, which is also called planet X, which is going to come in contact with the earth. This contact is going to shift the earth's poles and lead to flooding. It's set to happen on 9/23/17 in the afternoon.

I can send you a few links to YouTube videos, but this may happen. The good news is that where I live, in Missouri, we are safe. In fact, there's an underground facility near me that holds about 25,000 people. It's expected that all the high-ranking government officials will be here so that they will survive when the flooding occurs. I spent about $600 at Sam's club stocking up on food over the next few months. I need you to be here, Mike. Buy a plane ticket and be there by Friday night. I know this sounds ridiculous and I'm pretty sure it doesn't happen. But there's a tiny chance it might, but even if it doesn't we can still have an awesome weekend catching up."

As much as I wanted to tell Ben how absurd I thought this was, I had made a promise, and I wanted to keep it. Plus the YouTube videos were incredibly convincing and I thought it was possible the world could end. I bought a plane ticket that was overpriced since it was such late notice, but I was out there the night before the world was going to end. I had a slight sense of guilt, because although I was confident the world wasn't going to end, I wasn't 100 percent sure. I made no effort to tell any friends or family members about this. I could have at least sent those YouTube links my friend sent me.

As you may have expected, September 23, 2017 rolled around and the world did not end. But you should have seen how prepped my friend's house was. Spending $600 at Sam's club can get you a whole lot of beef jerky, protein bars, and Pop Tarts. I still enjoyed eating some of the doomsday delectables.

It was a fantastic weekend though. It helped me realize I don't always have to be so structured with how I live my life and can be spontaneous from time to time. Plus, he's a great friend. He thought the world might end, and forced me to give him an unconditional yes to make sure I was safe. Again, what a friend. A year later, this story helped me realize why we haven't succeeded as much as we thought we would by now.

We aren't willing to give an unconditional yes to something. We see the glamour in the goal attained, but neglect what it will take to attain it. I think of the movie *Cool Runnings,* a Disney movie about a Jamaican bobsled team starring John Candy as the bobsled coach, Irv. The following conversation is between Irv and one of the members of the Jamaican bobsled team, Sanka Coffie, played by Doug E. Doug. Sanka wants to be the driver, the most important position on the team because he believes he has the skill. Irv believes his teammate, Derrice, should be the driver.

Sanka: I'm the driver.

Irv: You're not. You're the brakeman.

Sanka: You don't understand, I am Sanka Coffie, I am the best pushcart driver in all of Jamaica! I must drive!

Irv: You see Sanka, the driver has to work harder than anyone. He's the first to show up, and the last to leave. When his buddies are all out drinking beer, he's up in his room studying pictures of turns. You see, a driver must remain focused one hundred percent at all times. Not only is he responsible for knowing every inch of every course he races, he's also responsible for the lives of the other men in the sled. Now, do you want that responsibility?

Sanka: I say we make Derice the driver.

Irv: So do I, Sanka. So do I.

Once Sanka saw the other side of what it would mean to be a driver, giving up drinking beer with his friends, having to work harder than everyone else, and carrying the responsibility of protecting his teammates' lives, he did not want to be the driver. I'm convinced you can't achieve greatness without sacrifice. Plus, you really don't know if you'll stay true to your commitment until you're tested.

Make the effort to look deeper into your dreams and goals. Because it's easy to focus on the benefits, and neglect to see the sacrifice. It's easy to be a "Sanka" in life, but it takes a little extra to be a "Derrice". To fulfill your divine purpose for why you're alive, you're going to have to say "Yes," to whatever it is, then ask, "what do I need to do right now to make this happen?"

Like most dreams, it isn't fun in the beginning. If you wanted to be a famous comedian like Kevin Hart, would you be willing to perform at a bar to crowds of ten people who are all heckling you? Would you be able to do this for ten years before you got your big break? Most aspiring comedians would say yes in the beginning, but the years of struggling and heckling often drains their spirit. Self-doubt creeps in and they lose hope. Eventually their heartache is no longer worth it and they settle for something more realistic.

Maybe you don't want to be a comedian. Maybe your dream is to be a doctor, lawyer, author, singer, or athlete. Whatever it is, you may be missing the other side, the grind, the struggle, the sacrifice needed to be successful. We think we are a Derrice, but once we learn what is being asked of us we turn out to be a Sanka.

I was able to give an unconditional yes to my friend, even though his request to fly out due to the world ending was ridiculous. How can we give an unconditional yes to our dreams?

Many dream and never act, some act but don't persist. What does it take to act on our dreams *and* persist? What does it take to give an unconditional yes to our life's mission and then ask, "What's the question?"

I thought for a while that it would take an "I'll show them," mentality. What I mean by this is someone out there is telling you it can't be done, or it will never happen so you shouldn't even try. I've actually had this play out a couple times in my life. The first time was when I was eight and at my Grandma's house. We had just finished eating *Shake 'n Bake* chicken and yellow rice, and we were moving on to dessert.

There were about 20 of us there. My grandma has been known to make some extraordinary cookies, but on this night, she brought out cookies *and* pie. My mom told me the greenish treat was key lime pie.

I shouted to my grandma, "Oh! Let me try it." "No, Michael. You won't like it." The dialogue between myself and my grandma over me trying this dessert went back and forth several times. Not to the point where it was heated, but it was starting to make the atmosphere uncomfortable. My dad chimed in, "Mom, just let him try it." "Fine, but he's not going to like it." As Granny slid me the slice of key lime pie, I wanted more than anything to love that pie, and prove that she was wrong.

Turns out I loved the pie! To this day it's my favorite. Is it because I actually like the sweet and sour tang of the pie, or that I was able to prove granny wrong? I really don't know. This example didn't really have a big impact on my life, but this "I'll show them" drive doesn't seem to be the way to achieve greatness *and* sustain it.

Let's say your dream is to run a successful key lime pie business. You are super passionate about it, and a close friend says, "It will never work, people will never be jazzed up about pies as much as you are." You were motivated, but this joker's comment has you even more fired up. You hustle and grind for years. You neglect your health, family, and commit your life to proving this person wrong.

I see this motive to prove someone wrong as a lose-lose for you. It's either you'll succeed or fail. If you fail, you weren't able to prove the person wrong and this may lead to you feeling devastated. If you succeed, maybe the person says, "Wow, you actually did it. I was wrong about you and key lime pies. Congrats." Maybe you think, "That's right! In your face!" It feels good for a while, but then this feeling of victory fades.

You may lose your drive, because this drive was based on proving someone wrong. You proved them wrong; now where's your motivation to keep going?

Your strongest motivation lies in your heart. A drive needs to come out of love. I think we struggle with what I call "Tin Man Troubles." This metaphor comes from *The Wizard of Oz*.

When young Dorothy first encounters the *Tin Man*, he responds, tight-lipped, "Oil can. Oil can." He explains after Dorothy oils him up that he got stiff, so stiff that he remained stuck where he was because his oil can was out of reach. At first glance it appears that a lack of oil was the Tin Man's problem. But when you think about it in a deeper way, oil was not the ultimate solution.

The tin man was lacking a heart. Just like in your life, easing your discomfort or removing your fear may seem like the ultimate solution, but that's just oil. The true solution to overcoming discomfort and fear is using your heart. Your heart can oil you from within. It provides intrinsic motivation.

The good news is that we are never lacking a heart. We need it to live. Our problem is that we aren't always using it. We get stiff in life, and this stiffness can come from having to do work that we don't like.

Derrice's driver duties in the movie *Cool Runnings* were being the first to show up and the last to leave. When his buddies are all out drinking beer, he's in his room studying pictures of turns. He needs to be focused one hundred percent at all times. Not only being responsible for knowing every inch of every course he races, but also responsible for the lives of the other men in the sled.

That kind of responsibility can make you stiff. You may be waiting on oil, which represents some motivation that makes you want to take on that responsibility, or perhaps a time when it's more convenient. However, this proverbial oil doesn't exist. These types of moments are a matter of the heart. If you're using your heart, you don't let responsibilities like this stiffen you from moving forward.

Maybe it's not responsibility, but lack of appreciation or validation. Over the past couple months I've been applying this tin man metaphor to my life. I had been going to church consistently for a few months and felt I should get more involved by volunteering in some aspect. The only problem is that all the volunteer duties made me stiff, they made me uncomfortable. Greeting people as they walk in? *I'm not really a greeting type of person. I'm more of a hang out in the corner and people watch type of person.* Working in the parking lot directing traffic? *Eh, I'm not really good at directing people. I would probably do more harm than good there.* Working in the kid's area? *I wouldn't be good there either. I don't have any kids, and I think some of the things I say would be too deep for a ten year old to understand anyway.*

You see, every volunteer duty I could do was making me stiff, and I thought oil was the problem. Maybe if I had more confidence greeting strangers, directing traffic, or working with kids, I wouldn't be so stiff. I believed I needed to feel comfortable, I needed to be oiled up, or I would be too stiff to contribute.

Then I realized it wasn't a matter of oil. It was a matter of the heart. When you're using your heart, you're willing to do what's asked of you. One day a woman, Valerie, with stylish purple hair, asked me to serve in the kid's area, and without hesitation I agreed. *What am I doing? This is not something I'm good at. This is something that I can't do!*

I answered myself with, *Michael, everything makes you stiff because the only thing you feel comfortable doing is hanging out at your house in your pajamas watching YouTube or writing stuff that you don't have the courage to share with others. You don't need oil. You don't have tin man troubles. You have a heart, just start using it.*

It's odd some of the pep talks I give myself, but this one worked for me. I thought my tin man troubles were behind me. In my mind, I was finally using my heart. I wasn't looking out for what was best for me. I was looking out what was best for what the church needed. Or so I thought.

I walked into the kid's area, and Valerie's husband, Tyler, who is a kind-hearted guy with an amazing beard, was serving in the kid's area with me that day. We were given the task of watching the kids between ages six and ten. The first activity involved us being put into teams and the first team to finish the puzzle won. There were about twenty kids in the room that day and Tyler announced, "Okay, let's break into teams. It's going to be my team and Michael's team." Three kids immediately shouted, "I want to be on your team, Tyler!" I was standing off in the corner and thinking, *I know you kids are seven, but how do you think this is making me feel? Why don't you want to be on my team?*

Tyler then said, "I'm going to break up the teams by one and twos. I'm one and Michael is two." Once again, several kids were dissing me, "I want to be on team one, I want to be on team one!" I still could not believe this was happening to me. I was using my heart and being somewhere I didn't want to be, and was being rejected. Tyler would say "One" to half the kids and their responses were more ecstatic than them receiving their favorite toy on Christmas.

The kids that were assigned my team, "two," had a depressed look on their face like their cat died. I almost felt like crying. I know they are kids, but I still couldn't believe that this was happening to me. Tyler was on the red carpet, and I was on the blue carpet. As the unfortunate kids who were "forced" to be on my team strolled over with frowns, I don't like the thought I had, but I had it. *Michael, these kids don't appreciate you, they don't want you here, you don't want to be here anyway. Just walk out. Just go home. You tried using your heart, but your heart isn't worth anything to them.* Have you ever had thoughts like these?

I had put my hand on the carpet and I was about to propel myself up and walk out the door when time seemed to freeze and something inside me was saying. "Your heart is being tested right now. You passed the first aspect of the test. You were willing to serve in an area that made you stiff, but now you need to see how you respond when you face what stiffens you and you don't receive appreciation for it. Who are you here for? If you're here for yourself, to have people appreciate you and tell you how wonderful you are, than leave. However, if you're truly here for these kids, then stay. Because it's not about how they feel about your service, it's about you being there to add value to their lives."

I wasn't super energetic because being around kids was out of my comfort zone, plus I also got dissed. But I shifted my focus, held back my tears, and did all the activities with those kids, hoping to add value to their lives. I'm grateful I stayed, and I'm grateful I didn't get up and walk out. It would have been an act of poor character.

Walking out could have led to me never doing something that made me stiff again, and could have prevented me from using my heart. However, staying leads me to doing the opposite.

With this book, no one may read it other than my mom. But I realize if I need validation from others to write, then I'm not using my heart. Using my heart would be sharing the love I have inside me in hopes of making your life better regardless of how it's received. It's easy for me to write this out, but it will be a challenge *to live it out*. Think about it. If you had a heart like this, almost nothing could stop you or make you stiff. You would be bold, courageous, and you would endure when everyone else who's not using their heart would quit.

I look at that time I volunteered in the kid's area, and once again, how I got dissed, as a blessing. It tested my heart. Many more heart tests will come and the same goes for you. But knowing you passed a tough test gives you confidence that you will be able to pass tougher heart-tests in the future. It can lead to you saying "yes" to your calling in life, and to keep answering your call, even when everything inside you wants to quit and pursue something that doesn't make you stiffen up so much.

I really think that's how you become great. You transcend the tin man troubles of getting stiff when it comes to responsibility, being fearful, or not having your love appreciated. You don't need oil, you don't need more confidence or appreciation. You just need to realize you have a heart and use it to love unconditionally.

Maybe that's why I gave my friend the unconditional yes and flew out to see him, even though his fear of the world ending seemed ridiculous. I was acting out of love. I wanted to be there for him and help him in whatever he needed. Maybe that's how some of your wildest dreams come true. They aren't out of you receiving validation and appreciation, or proving someone wrong, but using your heart.

I doubt tin man troubles will escape you completely. You may get stiff when someone is telling you that you can't do something. Fight that "I'll show them" urge. Don't pursue a key lime pie business just to show your granny how much you love key lime pie.

When someone is criticizing you, it's sometimes out of protection. They are trying to protect you so you don't get disappointed if your dreams don't pan out. Or, they are protecting themselves. If you go for it and succeed, then they will have to evaluate their life and wonder why they played it safe and didn't pursue their dreams.

You may get stiff when it comes to the non-glamourous aspects of becoming great, such as practicing and being patient in your development. It may cause you to make the choice Sanka did when it came to being the driver on the bobsled team. You may also get stiff when you use your heart and someone responds to you in a "thanks, but no thanks" manner, like the way those kids were feeling unfortunate being on my team. Getting stiff is normal. We want things to be easy and fun. We want to be appreciated and loved for who we are and what we do. To get more out of this metaphor, pretend to be the tin man when you realize you're getting stiff. Maybe extend out your arm and bend it, freeze in place, or get tight-lipped and say, "Oil can! Oil can!"

But remember, oil can loosen you up and get you moving again, but it's not your true issue. It's a matter of using your heart. If you get stiff, pause and reflect like I did when those seven-year-olds dissed me. Ask, "Who am I here for?" Remind yourself that you're not here for yourself. Visualize your heart beating and knowing you are not made of tin. I got a lot of fulfillment that day working with those kids who were forced on my team and with the smiles on their faces, they seemed okay being "stuck" on my team. I would have missed out on that moment if I didn't use my heart.

You're here to use that unique heart of yours in an extraordinary way. You're here to give an unconditional "yes" to the acts of service that are the dreams in your heart, the dreams that you're on this earth to fulfill. You've said yes, you realize you're not a tin man, you have a heart that can oil you from within, and you're going to use it. All you need to do now is ask, "What's the question?"

CHAPTER 10

TO BE GOOD OR HAVE FUN?

Some of the fondest memories I have as a kid were playing golf with my dad. When I was five, I had a plastic set of golf clubs and even remember riding in the golf cart while he played 18 holes. Once we got to the putting green on each hole, that's when I got to pretend to be a real golfer like my dad. I would drop my plastic ball a foot from the hole and putt the ball 10 times. Eventually it would go in.

Let's fast forward a bit. When I was 13, I overheard a conversation between my dad and his friend, Tommy. At this time in my life I was a husky kid, and was consistently hitting the ball farther than 300 yards. If you don't know golf well, just take my word for it, that's pretty far. I had a strange grip though. I held my clubs like a hockey stick, with several inches of space between my hands. This grip seemed to help me hit the ball far off the tee, but with hitting irons and chipping it caused me to miss the ball often.

My dad is a pretty good golfer. He has a handicap between five and ten. Tommy was a few strokes better than my dad. The three of us played several times, and Tommy was amazed that I was able to hit the ball with my wacky grip. Tommy saw the potential in me being a good golfer because of how far I could hit the ball, but he had doubts. He said on one tee box after we hit our drives, "You'll never be able to be consistent using the grip you're using."

I took a moment to process what Tommy said. Largely because he was a great golfer, and when someone more skilled than you gives you advice, it's wise to consider it. He then showed me how I should grip the club and then asked me to try hitting a ball. I shanked it badly and the grip felt so awkward. I tried hitting another ball and got the same result.

With this new grip, all my power was gone.

Tommy told me that it would take time to adjust, but if I wanted to be consistent, I had to change my grip. I tried it for a couple holes and every shot was terrible. I was no longer having fun. The following hole when Tommy was on the other side of the course was the perfect time to ask Dad without Tommy hearing. "Dad, do I really need to change my grip?" He took a few seconds then asked, "Son, do you want to be good or do you want to have fun?"

Without much hesitation I responded, "I want to be good!" "Son, then change your grip." Looking back, my dad's question was one of scarcity and limitations. It was a choice. You can be good and not have fun or you can have fun and not be good. My dad's question did not present an option where I could both be good *and* have fun.

My initial choice was to be good, so I stuck with Tommy's grip. I used it for several rounds with my Dad and Tommy. I was getting slightly better, but my power off the tee was gone. Driving the ball far was the most enjoyable part of golf for me. This new grip was making golf feel like a chore. I decided I wanted to have fun, more than I wanted to be good.

I went back to my whacky grip, crushing the ball off the tee. But, unfortunately, I was back to inconsistent swings. Sure, I was having fun, but I was feeling unfulfilled because I wasn't good. Truthfully, I have grown to despise golf because I believed it would only bring me fulfilment if I was good *and* having fun.

Eight years after my Dad's ultimatum, I was at my first day of Pharmacy School at the Medical University of South Carolina. One of my professors showed a slide with a similar choice.

The slide was titled, "Welcome to Pharmacy School." It then listed three bullet points:

-Sleep
-Good Grades
-Social Life

On the bottom of the slide was, "Pick two." Most of the class laughed, but I didn't. I was in deep contemplation considering my two options. *Well, I definitely need my beauty rest. I need to make sure I look refreshed when Mrs. Right comes along.* The choice was really between good grades and having a social life. I knew I would have to take out over $100,000 over the next four years to cover my tuition and I was terrified of socializing too much, having too much fun, and flunking out because of it.

I really didn't waver on my two picks over my time in pharmacy school. However, I did have a lot of regrets. For the most part, I went to the gym in the morning, once again to look good for Mrs. Right, went to class, then went home to study for about three hours. I got my sleep and got good grades, but didn't have much fun.

Since being out of school I've often wondered if I could have made a better selection. *Could I have chosen all three?* I could think of several classmates who were near the top of their class, seemed well rested, and had an enviable weekend Instagram feed. It would have been great to have the wisdom to realize that having all three was an option. It would have been a challenge, involving scheduling and discipline throughout the week, but it could have been done.

It's the same story with golf. I could have the option of being good *and* having fun, but my rules for fun would have to change. Instead of having fun and showing off driving the ball 300 yards, it could have been in making progress on my golf game, no matter how small the improvement.

Unless you own a time machine, you can't go back to your past, so it's not worth being bummed out by your choices. You made the best decision with what you had at the time. You see, in the past, my life was full of scarcity, "Be good *or* have fun?" "Good grades *or* social life?" And maybe yours is full of scarcity, too. "Excel at my career *or* be there for my family?" "Be in shape and eat bland food *or* be doughy and snack on Cool Ranch Doritos?"

The only problem with all these choices is that it's going to make you feel as if you're missing out. I can't speak for you, but I've used a lot of my creative brain power most of my life to make up excuses to stay in my comfort zone. Recently, I've considered using that power towards not choosing, but instead finding ways to have both.

I found myself almost going down the path of scarcity again with my student loans. I don't like that I have debt. I've set a goal that would have me paying off my student loan within three years, but it would require me to live with less extravagance. That means no expensive vacations like the cruise to Alaska my parents went on last year.

That means no more eating two tubs of Enlightened ice cream every day. It's a tasty, protein-packed sweet treat, but a pricey one: over $5 a container. Plus, it also means I would have to put my dream of publishing this book on hold. Publishing this book would cost me over $1,000 to edit, and to hire a good designer to make the cover look professional, that would be another $1,000. Last month, I made up my mind. Most of my paycheck would go towards getting out of debt, *then* I would pursue my dream.

The only problem is, I'm incredibly excited about this book. I'm constantly thinking about events in my life that taught me something. Maybe it just takes time for things to click for us. That's the case for me. My dad and my professor were genuinely trying to help. Their advice was realistic. However, by simply being provided a better question and using a little creativity, you may not have to choose. You could have both.

As I boiled down my latest decision, it was between paying this specific monthly student loan payment to have my loan paid off in three years *or* lowering the payment to afford the cost required to get this book in your hands. I initially chose making the loan payment, but delaying my dream was draining my soul. The other day I shifted my thought to lowering my monthly payment in order to publish this book. I thought, *being in debt is no big deal. As 21st century philosopher and rapper Drake once said, "You only live once. It's the motto."*

But this choice wouldn't be fulfilling either. I want to be responsible and pay what I owe quickly. But one question popped into my mind that was a game changer. How can you keep your loan payment where it is *and* have the money to publish the book? I was immediately flooded with answers. *You could play the lotto or buy scratch-offs? No, you've tried that strategy and that's wishful thinking. You could ask someone rich for the money? No, that's not the answer either because you would then feel obligated to pay them back.* Then I found the answer.

I've had the opportunity to get paid overtime at work, and I've decided to do it. This month I am going to have extra shifts than I'm normally used to working, but this option allows me to pay my student loan off in three years *and* have money for the book. Plus, I may even have some money left over for a pint or two of the Red Velvet Cake-flavored *Enlightened* ice cream.

Living a life of abundance and possibilities requires sacrifice. Yes, I'm a little tired after working 58 hour work weeks, but my excitement level is off the charts knowing I didn't have to choose. I could be responsible and disciplined with my loans *and* create this book! I'm grateful that I learned this lesson and started asking better questions. I hope you start doing the same.

When I was 13 I could have asked, "How can I be good *and* have fun?" The answer I have now is to celebrate every time I make progress and look at every opportunity out on the golf course as an opportunity to bond with someone. Plus, my grip was unusual, but maybe it could have worked. After, all, if you've seen the movie *Happy Gilmore*, starring Adam Sandler, you'll recall his character won the golf championship gripping his clubs like a hockey player.

When I was entering pharmacy school I could have asked, "How can I get my sleep, get good grades, *and* have a social life?" Again, with limited effort I could have gotten into a study group with a couple guys and could have socialized *and* studied at the same time. I could have gone to the gym with my classmates, getting sculpted for Mrs. Right *and* socializing at the same time. Plus, I could have asked a pretty girl in my class to be my lab partner, and improved my chemistry both in a science *and* a romantic sense.

Again, removing the scarcity and limitations when it comes to approaching these choices can lead to answers that make you feel giddy. I cannot begin to tell you how excited I am right now, because I realize there's potential solutions out there where you don't have to choose. You can find ways to have both.

What about you? I imagine there's some passion or skill you have that you enjoy. What would it take for you to keep enjoying it *and* getting better at it? How could you improve to the point that you could make a living off of it? As far as your work-life balance, what would it take to excel at your career *and* be there to spend quality time with your family?

Sorry to break it to you, but in order to have both, you may have to give up something good. But as Stephen R. Covey, the late author of the classic book, *The Seven Habits of Highly Effective People*, once said, "Sacrifice really means giving up something good for something better."

Today, I did have to give up something good, watching YouTube videos to instead write this chapter. But, writing this chapter was better and brought me much more fulfillment than YouTube. Sometimes you won't be able to have both. You can't lie *and* tell the truth. You can't take advice from the devil *and* angel on your shoulder. You can't be a person of poor *and* high character. As long as the choice doesn't corrupt your character, try using your creativity to have both. You can't physically be at work *and* your friend's poetry reading, but ask yourself how to make both happen anyway. Asking could lead to you being able to reschedule something at work to be at your friend's poetry reading.

There is another side to ultimatums, and that's not having to have them at all. It likely will require you to sacrifice something good, but it will make room for something *better*. Give this question serious thought: Why not use your creative brain power to ask the question that removes scarcity, removes limitations, and allows you to make a truly fulfilling choice?

CHAPTER 11

THE MISSING PIECE

If I gave you a puzzle to work on and told you it would be a pretty picture, but there's one piece missing, I doubt you would waste your time working on this puzzle. No matter how many of the jumbled pieces you got in order, and no matter how beautiful the picture looked, if it couldn't be completed, you wouldn't be fully satisfied.

This morning I googled "world record for puzzle with the most pieces". If you had to guess, how many pieces would you think? I thought maybe 20,000, but my guess was way off. According to Guinness World Records, the jigsaw puzzle with the most pieces had 551,232 pieces! It took 1,600 students working together to complete the puzzle.

Imagine if this group of 1,600 students spent all this time working on the puzzle and were missing that last piece. To have 551,231 out of the 551,232 pieces in the right place. If the last piece of this puzzle was the only piece missing, it would be 99.999819 percent complete. These 1,600 students put in the work to complete the puzzle because they assumed all the pieces were there. They were willing to put in the work because they believed they could have it 100 percent completed.

What can make you even more unhappy is looking at the person who has the missing piece you're looking for. You think, *if I could have what they have, my life would be complete.*

Can you think of a time you found yourself envious of someone, wishing you could trade lives with them? This past year I found myself doing this. I know I have a lot to be grateful for. I'm in good health, I have a job that pays well, an amazing family, and many wise people in my life who've taught me priceless lessons. But it's tough to focus on all that's present in your life when you're reminded of what's missing.

I was reminded of what was missing in my life after attending my best friend's wedding.

I had just turned 27 and was nowhere close to being married. A couple months after the wedding, I went to visit him in his new five-bedroom house with fancy columns in the front.

My friend and I were alone in his kitchen and I decided it was time to start the pity party. I let out a deep sigh, "Man, I wish I had your life. You're married, *and* you have a house with fancy columns." He laughed at first, and it's likely because having columns in front of your house seemed to be more important to me than just about everyone else. But his laugh was followed by a sigh, "Mike, I wish I had *your* life."

It took me a few seconds to process what I just heard before responding, "What?! Why would you want *my* life?" "Mike, I want your hair. My hair is thinning and I'd love to have a thick brown mane like you." I busted out laughing, because I don't think anyone had ever complimented me on my hair before. I never thought about it; in fact, I rarely combed it.

I told my friend, "You've got to be kidding me. It's just hair!" What he said back got me thinking deeply. "Mike, it's easy for you to say that when you have it." I didn't go to bed until 2 a.m. that night because I was struggling to comprehend our conversation of me in envy of his life and him in envy of mine. He had the missing piece in *my* life, but he seemed just as eager to switch places with me because I had a missing piece in *his.*

I pondered deeply that night in a way I never had before and thought, *maybe your missing piece is not going to complete you. This piece could eventually be present in your life, but you'd likely still feel incomplete because your focus would shift to something else missing in your life.* For example, you may get married, but then the missing piece shifts to having children, then the piece may shift to having the free time you did before having kids, before being married.

On the puzzle of our lives, we often focus on what's missing and strive to complete the picture. There is another side that we tend to miss: *the pieces that are already there.* When you focus on all that's present in your life, it becomes difficult to feel unsatisfied and incomplete.

Deep down I knew that if I didn't change my focus, my life would be filled with blessings but I would never be able to appreciate them. The dominant question I had throughout my life up until this conversation with my friend was, "What's missing?" Because that's what I focused on, I always came up with answers. It was often what others had that I didn't, whether it was a trampoline, a college degree, a marriage; and throughout life I would keep finding missing pieces.

I realized that if you don't like your life, maybe all you need to do is change what you're focusing on. It was 1:06 a.m. and I thought, *It's time to change my focus. I'm going to stop looking for what's missing, I'm now going to focus on what's already here.*

I tiptoed to the guest bathroom that night and glanced at the mirror to focus on my hair. Trying to hold in my laughter I thought, *I can't believe my friend would trade lives with me over my hair.* I had never taken the time to admire my hair, but after what my friend said I started to appreciate a puzzle piece in my life I took for granted. It also occurred to me that with each piece you gain you often have to give up one you take for granted.

For example, maybe you get married and have kids, but with that you give up free time to do the things you want to do. Maybe you get a sculpted physique, but then have to give up pepperoni pizza Hot Pockets. Maybe you gain fame, but then you have to give up your privacy, you can no longer go to Walmart and buy pepperoni pizza Hot Pockets without being hounded by fans for pictures and autographs.

Really think about the missing piece in your life. If you continue to believe you need to have this piece in your life to be happy, you'll forfeit every second in your present moment waiting on happiness. It seems ridiculous to me now that we do this. Why not embrace the circumstances in our lives *right now*, being grateful for the present pieces and not letting the missing ones depress us?

I decided it was time to take responsibility and make the effort to shift what I was focusing on.

The following morning over breakfast I saw my friend and his wife holding hands and were being lovey dovey to the point it makes you nauseous.

My old reaction would have been, "I deserve someone like this in my life too, it's not fair!" This morning I was thinking, *I'm done being jealous of people having what I don't have. He's my friend, and I'm happy he's married. Plus, mom says I'm a catch and I'll meet that special girl any day now. Plus she promised me she wasn't just saying that because I'm her son, even though I still have my doubts if she really means it.* What if you do the same? The next time you have a friend, or even your mom, tell you that you have a lot going for you, entertain the possibility that what they said was true.

Instead of asking "What's missing?" and frantically searching for it like it was the last piece of my puzzle, I finally found myself at peace. I finally took the time to break my life into pieces that I take for granted every day, and I realized I had so many pieces already in place. I have a nice thick, brown mane on the top of my head, a car that runs, legs that walk, a laptop to type out stories that forever change my life, a roof over my head, a bed of my own, a family who loves me. I know I could go on and on, and when you think about how blessed *you already are* you may be brought to tears. It makes what's missing in your life an afterthought.

My friend, I promise that whatever you think is missing in your life, obtaining it will *never* complete you. You'll find that piece, then find someone who has more than you and you'll fixate on something new that's missing. Stop wishing to trade places with someone. They may have pieces that you are missing in your life, but don't forget that you have pieces missing in theirs.

You can work hard your whole life and acquire more pieces than anyone; you could even own the record for most pieces with 551,233, but if the picture in your mind's eye is one short of being complete, you'll never be at peace. The other side I now see is that you are a product of what you focus on. Stop focusing on what others have and the missing piece in your life. Focus on what's already present in your life and more pieces will be present than you realize.

CHAPTER 12

BEAR ATTACKS

There's a night shirt my grandma wore often that can forever change your life

It was teal night shirt with pink lettering that said, "No, No, No, No, No, No, No....Well, Maybe." I didn't give it much thought back then, but I do now. In this scenario on granny's night shirt, what is this person asking for? A date? A loan? For the person to listen to their mixtape in hopes of getting a record deal?

Whatever they're asking for it must be important because getting a "no" from someone often crushes your spirit. We don't know how the dialogue unfolds. All we know is that this individual has tried seven times, has gotten a no each time, and on attempt number eight, still hasn't gotten a "yes." I think we're expecting yeses in life too fast and have an exaggerated fear on a potential no. Think of how hopeful this person on my grandma's nightshirt became with the pause and "Well, maybe" reply. After so many no's, "Well, maybe" implies possibility and it raises hope that you're not wasting time. After so many no's, "Well, maybe" encourages you to keep trying.

I'm realizing your *interpretation* of what's happening in your life is more important than what is *actually happening*. One great example is from a scene in the movie *Dumb and Dumber* starring Jim Carrey. Jim Carrey plays Lloyd Christmas, a chip-toothed limousine driver, who immediately falls in love with Mary Swanson, a woman he drove to the airport.

To most it would seem Mary is out of Lloyd's league, that Lloyd is wasting time even pursuing her. Maybe it's courage, or stupidity, but Lloyd asks about his chances with being with Mary.

Lloyd: What are my chances?
Mary: Not good.
Lloyd: You mean not good like 1 out of 100?
Mary: I'd say more like 1 out of a million

There's a seven second pause where he's processing what he just heard, appearing to be devastated before he puts on a huge grin and says, "So you're telling me there's a chance?" With a smile still plastered on his face he then shouts "Yeah!"

I imagine if someone told you the odds of doing what you wanted to do was 1 in a million, you'd likely give up and pursue something more realistic. Please don't get me wrong, I'm not telling you that you can do *anything* you put your mind to. But your odds of succeeding at *almost everything* increases dramatically when you interpret events differently.

In our *Dumb and Dumber* example, maybe Lloyd could eventually win Mary's heart with his persistence, but maybe not. Maybe he's not her type and never will be. However, I strongly believe there are many hopes and aspirations that are possible and your odds will increase dramatically *if you interpret things differently.*

Let's bring up why you don't go for what you want. It's likely because there's a high chance you believe you'll get a "no". This no can represent rejection, criticism, or failure of some sort. Psychologists tell us we are more fearful of a potential loss than hopeful for a potential gain. We often avoid potential losses at all costs and we handle them like bear attacks.

Let's pretend you're out hiking in a forest in Montana and you come across a 1,000-pound grizzly bear. This is something you were not anticipating, but it's within a hundred feet of you and your mission is to survive the bear's potential attack. What do you do? Play dead, right? You lie on the ground. You're still, silent, and fearful. You hope it doesn't notice you, and if it does, that it senses no life in you and passes you by.

This scenario isn't likely to happen, but our minds create imaginary bears that are trying to attack us. These imaginary bears could represent people rejecting and criticizing you for pursuing a dream that seems unrealistic. They could represent potential heartbreak and disappointment when you fail and your dreams don't work out. Your imaginary bear is any fear holding you back from being fully alive. What is *your* imaginary bear? What is making you so fearful that you're playing dead in life? Being rejected and criticized by others? Feeling like a failure? Seriously, answer what your bear is before moving on so you can overcome it.

I'm not sure if playing dead with a real grizzly bear is the answer, but playing dead is *never* the answer in life. When we play dead in life, we are jealous and criticize others who are pursuing their dreams. We tell ourselves and others that we don't care, when we secretly care deeply. We wake up breathing and eating, but never feel like we're living.

Keep in mind that your fears are in your head. They are imaginary bears. Mary telling Lloyd, "This will never happen, not even in your dreams," may cause him to be depressed and devastated for a couple months, but it's not going to kill him. Plus as painful as rejection and failure are, they pale in comparison to the pain of regret.

Playing dead to *survive* life takes minimal effort compared to attempting to *thrive* in life. Plus, it appears this bear attack idea helped Marissa, a friend of mine, to realize that playing dead isn't the answer to overcoming her fears. She sent me this message.

"I've been back and forth on whether or not to pursue a residency in veterinary pharmacy- it's super competitive: 3 schools in the country offer it and there's a total of 5 spots. There's a chance I won't get one of those 5 spots but I definitely won't get one if I play dead and don't try at all. Further, I've been with my current company for 6 years now but I'm actively trying to find some sort of job in the veterinary world that would hopefully help me in the long run to get one of the five spots (even if it means giving up my current job). Anyway, if you would've asked me a month ago about this, I would've said no way am I going to put myself out there for one of 5 spots and no way would I quit my current job after being there all this time but I'm 100% going for it now!!"

Let's break down what was preventing Marissa from going after what she really wanted. In her mind, the odds of getting one of those five spots were slim, maybe 1 in a 100, but she realized playing dead and not even trying leads to the odds being impossible. She also mentioned a potential "sunk cost". She had invested six years with her current employer. Losing what you already have is another potential bear. We often will stay where we are not because it's what we truly want, but because we've invested so much into it and are afraid of losing it. This is another form of playing dead: *not moving from where you are for fear of losing what you already have.*

Whether or not Marissa gets the job is secondary to the change in her thinking when it comes to going after what's important to her. She was able to acknowledge her doubts about her chances, acknowledge her fear of losing her current job, and still go for it anyway. She realized if she doesn't give herself a chance because of what's at stake if it doesn't work out, she'll be playing dead and she'll never be able to truly live. This new mentality will radically increase her chances of making her dreams a reality.

THE OTHER SIDE OF LIFE

We even see these fears played out in the movie *Shrek*, an animated movie about an ogre played by Mike Myers. Shrek's precious solitude is suddenly shattered by an invasion of annoying fairy tale characters. His mission was to restore this solitude by removing everyone from his swamp.

Shrek may act like his life is perfect, but being isolated, alone in a swamp, keeping others away with a sign that says "KEEP OUT" is a way to avoid what he really wants. Like everyone, Shrek wants to be loved and accepted, but he's defined by his society to be ugly, scary, and incapable of love, a story he's told himself over the years and a story he believes.

His sign that says "KEEP OUT" is Shrek's way of avoiding the pain of rejection he's been experiencing his whole life. It's his way of playing dead and avoiding potential bear attacks. It's much easier for us to tell ourselves a story that we love our life, so that we can stay where we are and avoid negative consequences of being unsuccessful going after what we really want. Fortunately, later on in the movie Shrek reveals the truth to Donkey, and Princess Fiona overhears him. If he didn't take a closer look at himself and open up to others about how he really felt, he would have never gotten the love and acceptance he needed.

Can you imagine if Shrek was never honest with himself for fear of how he really felt? He likely would have been depressed and all alone in his swamp. No marriage, no kids...and no sequels for us to see. Pretty sad indeed. Are *you* doing the same thing? Are you telling yourself a story like Shrek did to play dead and avoid the bear attacks you create in your mind?

Again, I do want to point out that there are no guarantees that your dream will come true if you never give up. However, I will say that if your dream is about something larger than yourself, something that will make the world a better place, then pursuing it is not a waste of your life.

Sometimes what seems unrealistic can actually be realistic if you persist. Let's go back to my grandma's shirt. The first time the person asked for something and got a "No," it would be realistic to think, *I asked and they weren't interested. I guess it wasn't meant to be.* But I'd argue it could also be realistic to think, *This idea is so bizarre and something this person has never seen before. Plus, this is the first time I'm pitching it. Maybe I can go home and work on delivering a more simple and persuasive pitch, one that highlights the benefits they'll receive from saying yes to my offer.*

Maybe you believe strongly in what you're doing and spend several years working on your pitch, sharpening your skills, and you've gotten a million "no's". You can once again change your thinking and believe this thought is realistic, *Rejection does sting a bit, but it's an imaginary bear attack, it can never kill me. I also believe with all my heart that I'm going after this because the people who say yes to this will have their life positively enriched. Plus, I'm thrilled that although I haven't succeeded yet, I'm not playing dead. I care deeply, I have passion towards this, and I'm willing to accept the possibility of looking foolish, being criticized, and having others misunderstand me to make this happen and truly thrive in life.*

My friend, when you are about to quit on something that matters to you, take your focus off the "yes" you haven't gotten yet and focus on a "Well, Maybe". This is a sign of progress. This is when people pause and reevaluate you and think, I'm still not sure, but maybe it's not as crazy as I initially thought. Perhaps the "Well, Maybe" is a personal milestone. The first time I gave a motivational speech in front of an audience without my lip nervously twitching like Elvis was my own "Well, Maybe".

I thought, *It may take years or even decades to master the art of speaking, but my lips didn't twitch! I have a ton of work ahead of me, but I'm closer than the day before!* This small progress shifted me from "no" to "Well, Maybe" and encouraged me to keep trying.

I believe deep within you, you have an aspiration that appears to be 1 in a million like Lloyd's chances with Mary, but the odds seem impossible because of your imaginary bears.

However, if you believed that these bears were imaginary, playing dead would seem silly to you. Don't forget that we all have fears. It's easy to appear fearless when you play dead and never courageously pursue anything.

Your odds can raise dramatically by overcoming these bears. For example, let's say there are 1,000 people across the country that want the veterinary job Marissa wants. I'm confident most of those thousand people are having this internal dialogue, *There's no way someone like me would get this. Someone way more qualified and with a better resume will get it. Applying is a waste of my time. I'll just be setting myself up for disappointment applying and thinking I have a shot.*

So out of these 1,000 people who want this, most of them talk themselves out of it and don't even try out of fear of being rejected. Their grizzly bears cause them to play dead. You see, most people play dead with their dreams and never try. You being courageous, daring to live by simply trying gives yourself a chance, and the odds are often better than you think.

This happened to me in college with a $500 scholarship from *Flander's Butt Paste*. Yes, this is a *real* product and a *real* scholarship. I thought, *someone like me would never get this. I'm just an average guy and I don't have any inspiring stories to convince them that I should get this scholarship.* However, then I thought, *there's a chance everyone is thinking this and almost no one is submitting an application for this scholarship. What do I have to lose? I'll give it a shot.*

Three weeks later I received an email from *Flander's Butt Paste* congratulating me for winning the scholarship. From time to time I'll walk down the baby aisle at grocery stores and see that butt paste and use it as a reminder to overcome my fears and doubts and give myself a chance by going for it.

Like the person on my granny's night shirt, It's possible that the first time you try, it doesn't work out. It's possible you keep trying and get six more nos. Maybe on attempt number seven you want to quit, but because you know playing dead is not the answer, you try once more. You get a long pause followed by, "Well, Maybe." Maybe your optimism is low after the "Well, Maybe" because they are telling you it's a one-in-a-million chance.

But remember, if you never try it's always going to be a "no". If you give up, it's always going to be a "no". Also remember, a "yes" isn't what makes a life worth living. What makes life worth living is overcoming your imaginary bears that have caused you to play dead. What makes life worth living is acknowledging your doubts, acknowledging your fears, and going for your dreams anyway. You do this, and when it comes to getting the most out of life, I'm telling you there's a chance!

CHAPTER 13

WHAT HONEY BEES TEACH YOU

I was heading out the door one Thursday to meet a friend at Subway. Subway is my go-to place for meeting people and I get the same thing every time, a footlong turkey on toasted whole wheat bread with lettuce, tomatoes, and jalapenos. I locked my front door with that sandwich on my mind, but before I could get to my car there was an extreme pain in my left ear.

Something had stung me. I flicked the insect, which turned out to be a honey bee, off my ear and noticed my ear was turning red and swelling. Laugh at me if you want, but I almost cancelled my lunch date because of the discomfort. I ended up going because I try to honor all my commitments, plus I wanted that turkey sub.

I wondered if what I heard was true, that if a bee uses its stinger to sting someone, it will kill itself in the process. As it turns out, this is true for the honey bee. When a honey bee stings a person, it cannot pull its barbed stinger back out. It leaves behind not only the stinger, but also part of its abdomen and digestive tract, plus muscles and nerves. The massive rupture kills the honey bee as it tries to fly away.

A honey bee will sting when it perceives a threat to its hive, but when it's away from the hive foraging, it will rarely sting anyone unless someone steps on it or handles it roughly.

Believe it or not, stinging innocent people who are just trying to have a delicious sub at Subway and bond with a friend is not a honey bee's main objective. Their main task is to cultivate honey. Honey bees make honey by visiting flowers. They collect sugary juice called nectar from the blossom by sucking it out with their tongue. Bees have glands which secrete an enzyme that mixes with the nectar in the bee's mouth that turns the nectar into honey. What the bee collects, it stores back at the beehive in honeycombs.

I give you all this information because we can use it to compare ourselves to honey bees when it comes to our words. We have to be careful how we use our words. As highlighted in this well-known proverb, "The tongue has the power of life and death, and those who love it will eat its fruit." -Proverbs 18:21 NIV.

Just like honey bees, we have the ability to use hurtful words that act like stingers that can cause a great deal of pain to others, but lead to our death. However, we also have the ability to use our words to encourage, inspire, and appreciate others, which produces honey and makes the world a sweeter place.

Why do people waste their lives using hurtful words? Why would they commit their life to stinging others and miss out on living a great life in the process?

When I was a senior in high school I was eating at a Chick-fil-A with one of my best friends, Chase. He went to a different school than me, so we would often hang out with friends from his school whom I didn't know well. During lunch that Tuesday afternoon one of his friends, Jacob, approached our table. Jacob was probably 6'5, athletic, and seemed very excited about something. "Chase, I just heard from Lynchburg College. They're offering me a full-ride soccer scholarship!" "Congrats, Jacob! I'm not surprised. You're the best player on our team," Chase responded.

While observing their conversation without showing expression on my face I thought, *Their school soccer team must be terrible. Why is this guy so excited to go to a school no one's ever heard of?* After Chase and Jacob talked for another minute, Chase introduced me to Jacob. It was nothing out of the ordinary, a generic handshake and "Nice to meet you" from both of us. Jacob then left Chick-fil-A so filled with joy that he was almost skipping.

Once Jacob was free and clear I decided to weigh in with Chase about how I felt about Jacob's good news. "*Lynchburg? Pssh. that's probably a division 3 school,*" I said with my arms crossed, with an unimpressed tone and facial expression. With a look of disgust, Chase fired back, "Why didn't you say that to his face?" The smirk I had on my face was now gone. Chase glared at me for five seconds before asking another question, "Mike, where's your scholarship?" I now had a lot of shame for what I said. I was trying to tear Jacob's accomplishment down to feel better about myself, but now felt even worse.

Looking back now, I know why I didn't say what I said to Jacob's face. First off, I have never been in a fight my whole life and didn't want Jacob to knock my teeth out.

More importantly, I didn't say to Jacob what I told my friend because I had no problem with Jacob. The problem was with *me*. I was jealous. Jacob had something worth bragging about and I didn't. I saw his success as a threat to my self-image. Like a honey bee, I tried to sting Jacob because I thought he was a threat to my hive.

Before saying those mean words about Jacob I subconsciously told myself, *Oh no! Someone who is getting more attention and has more success than you, you can't have that. Quick! Find a way to tear him down to feel better about yourself.* What's odd is I don't play soccer. It's not like Jacob getting a soccer scholarship took away a spot I was looking to have on a college soccer team somewhere.

If this is the case, why did I feel threatened by this news in Chick-fil-A that day? More importantly, why do you feel threatened when *you* hear news of someone succeeding? Why couldn't I just be happy for Jacob and give him kind words about his success?

Maybe because I believed success was scarce. If someone else has success, that means there's less for us and we can't be successful. If we don't have their success, how can we look ourselves in the mirror and be happy with what we see? There are a select few who have no problem bashing people straight to their face, but a majority do so behind their backs like I did, either sharing their opinion with someone else, or just by having these jealous thoughts about others and not sharing them.

I'm grateful Chase confronted me that day. It caused me to drastically reduce the amount of negative criticism I shared with others. However, I still had stinger-like thoughts. *She probably cheated to score an A on that test. He's more successful than me because he's brown-nosing his boss. They are just lucky and know the right people.*

I can give you countless examples, but after years of jealousy and having thoughts of putting others down to feel better about myself, I realized it wasn't improving my life. My words and thoughts were acting like the bee's stinger, having the ability to hurt others, but ultimately hurting myself the most.

My strategy wasn't working and I figured the opposite would. I committed to being genuinely happy for other people's success even if their success caused me to feel inadequate. Whether it was friends getting married when I was still single, friends getting promotions that led to them making more money than me, or anything else, I was going to share my honey. "That's fantastic! You two deserve each other." "Congrats, you worked hard and earned that promotion!" were responses that people started hearing from me.

It felt really sweet to use these words. I was feeling so good, I even challenged myself to start complimenting people. I thought about the people in my life and about what I admired in them to the point of jealousy. Whether it be their chiseled physique, sense of humor, or their brilliance, instead of bad mouthing them in my head, I decided to compliment them *to their face*.

My compliments made them smile, and made me smile as well. Then I realized that a lot of people have self-doubt and are too critical of themselves. I made the effort to encourage people whenever I could. Once again, using kind words felt so sweet. I make the effort not to judge people when they say hurtful things about others, often behind their backs, because I've done it myself.

Author Will Bowen has said, "Hurt people hurt people." Those four words can have a powerful effect on you and cause you to be more compassionate. Let's use my example with Jacob. I cowardly said those hurtful words behind his back, because I was hurting. I had low self-esteem and didn't see myself as able to achieve success in my own life. This belief made me want to use my stinger to take out threats to my ego instead of sharing honey.

Think about someone who bullied you in your earlier years. Studies confirm that over 80 percent of us have been victimized by our peers at some point in our childhoods. Did you deserve it? Probably not. The bully did it because he or she was hurting. Maybe it was from some insecurity kept hidden, or maybe they thought they had to put you down to lift themselves up. Whatever the reason, they were hurting in some way.

Looking at people who are saying hurtful things to you with compassion helps you handle their words like the honey bee that stung me that day. Their words can still sting, and temporarily slow you down, but they can't kill you. The pain goes away, and ends up doing more harm to them when you let it go and move on with your life.

In the book *Popular* by Mitch Prinstein, he teaches you the two different types of popularity. One is status. This is being the best, having power, and being special in some way. Status is something we all seem to covet, but the author explains this type of popularity ultimately leads to dissatisfaction and depression. The other type of popularity is likability. This is the one that leads to your greatest happiness.

The author explains, "Prioritizing likability over status means choosing to help others rather than exclusively satisfying our own needs, showing more interest in others rather than vying for attention and power, and cultivating relationships more than "likes."

Let's go back to my example with Jacob. In that moment when I tried to diminish his accomplishment, I was seeking status. I wasn't trying to satisfy *his* need of praise with kind words, but satisfying *my own* with a put down. I was trying to vie for attention and power instead of taking advantage of an opportunity to make a new friend by congratulating him.

Later on in the book, *Popular*, which I highly recommend, the author provides an acronym that fits in perfectly with this chapter. The author said the goal to be more likable at work is to cultivate a H.I.V.E. - which stands for a group that feels Happy, Included, Valued, and Engaged.

I've learned death and life really are in your words. Your hurtful words can lead you to feeling dead inside, or your words that make others feel happy, included, valued, and engaged lead you to being more popular as well as feeling more alive on the inside. Being a "hater" never heals your hurting. It's only when you put your stinger away and commit to sharing honey that your life changes for the better.

Make sure your words are sincere and not flattering. Let's think of a scenario where I'm an employee of yours and compliment your fashion sense. It makes you feel incredible. Five seconds go by and then I ask you if I can borrow twenty dollars and leave an hour early. Turns out my compliment isn't so sweet because I had an ulterior motive.

We also need to make sure that our sweet words are followed by sweet actions. Turns out you can lie. You can say beautiful things and not mean any of them. In high school, I took an elective class, Medical Terminology, that was taught by Mrs. Stewart, which only had eight students. There were seven gorgeous aspiring nurses, and me. It was my favorite class. All the girls would playfully flirt with me, but I never knew what to say. I often turned as red as a rose. Valentine's day was coming up and I thought it would be sweet of me to buy Mrs. Stewart and the seven beauties a rose.

However, money was tight back in those days, as I was making $5.50 an hour bagging groceries, and I decided against buying the roses. But the *thought* of the roses for the women in that class was so beautiful and I wanted to cash in on it. I walked into class that morning and Hannah, the captain of the cheerleading squad smiled at me and said, "Happy Valentine's Day, Michael." I blushed like I always did, but as all the girls were focusing on me I managed to get these words out.

"Ladies, I wanted to buy each one of you a rose," I continued with a deep sigh, "But, I didn't have any money." I heard a collective "awe," and throughout the week all the girls mentioned how sweet I was. For years I would go back and revisit that moment and feel like a wonderful guy. However, now I revisit that moment with disappointment. I now realize that if I wasn't able to buy the roses for the girls I should have kept that thought for myself. Whenever I'm about to share a nice thought or intention I want to think, "Show them the honey." It's a mantra that can help you share kind words only if you're willing to back them up with actions.

For example, if you say to a friend, "If you are ever going through a tough time, you can come over anytime and we can talk." They can think you're a great friend. Then one day they get fired from work and want to come over. You have a date at Subway, and you're not willing to break your amazing dinner plans to be there for your friend. Based on your actions, you didn't mean what you said. Like me in Mrs. Stewart's class, you were using your words to appear sweet, but had no intention of showing them the honey.

I challenge you to put away your stinger. Stop being jealous of others and be happy for them instead. Commit your life to being a sweet talker with your kindness, admiration, and encouragement by remembering to use your H.I.V.E. Make others around you happy, included, valued, and engaged. And lastly, mean what you say. It's pretty sad those eight women didn't get a rose from me on that Valentine's Day back in high school, but I've learned my lesson. Before we move one, remember this, live your life using your words the way honey bees are intended to live: cultivating honey and making the world a sweeter place.

CHAPTER 14

THE OTHER SIDE
OF THE FINISH LINE

If you are in the top one percent in anything, you're a pretty big deal. Is there anything you feel you're in the top one percent in? Maybe it's your looks, intelligence, or a random skill like your ability to dominate in the board game *Monopoly*.

Any area where you are in the top one percent tends to make you feel special, but what if you aren't shining in any areas of your life? You probably are trying to find something. In my early twenties, I was still trying to find something that made me feel like I mattered, something that would impress everyone.

I was in the gym with my good friend Chris lifting weights one afternoon when he asked me a question, "Mike, have you ever run a marathon?" "No way! I would never run 26 miles, that's insane!" I replied. Then Chris said something that I'll never forget, "I heard less than one percent of the world has run a marathon."

And just like that, I had a burning desire to run a marathon, because doing so would put me in the top one percent of something. What was really exciting was that long distance running wasn't much about talent or how fast you were; it was more about endurance. If you're willing to push through the pain and endure, then you could run a marathon.

Around that same time it hit me that your grades in college could work the same way. It's easy to make straight A's when you're a genius, but you have a chance of doing well in school if you're willing to endure, to study several hours a day.

My daily routine changed because I believed that I could be in the top one percent if I was willing to put in the work. All of a sudden I was running close to 70 miles a week to build up my endurance, and I was studying three hours *every* day in hopes of making straight A's.

I became super intense about my diet, too. I'd even skip dinner with my friends or family because I didn't want to eat junk food. I wanted to have chia seed, oatmeal protein smoothies to properly fuel my runs. On weekends I didn't want to spend time with anyone, I just wanted to do my long runs and study.

My hope was that if I did well in school, I'd set myself up for a great future, and I'd be in the top one percent in life. As for the marathon, I had been training for over six months intensely and in 2012 signed up to run the Kiawah Island Marathon in South Carolina. The day of the marathon arrived and on that Saturday December morning I left the house at 5am. The race was an hour's drive away, so I wanted to make sure I was early.

The temperature was in the early 50s, and I made sure to pack my iPod shuffle. I never ran without it. It seemed there were a thousand people running that race and many were conversing with each other, but I wasn't. Back then I was quiet and reserved, especially on this day. I was all business. I got my racing number and went back into my car to wait for the next hour before the race started.

8 A.M. rolled around and I could see a giant clock counting down the race start time, which was now under five minutes. I did some brief stretching and pulled out my iPod to find a good song to get me going. I was thinking "Eye of the Tiger" by the band Survivor. I turned on my iPod and heard a voice that I wished I didn't, "Battery low." *No! This can't be! Not now! I need music to run. How will I find the motivation to keep going without music?*

I found the motivation partly out of fear. I would have been embarrassed to fail and not reach the finish line after working so hard. Can you relate to this, pushing yourself to avoid others judging you as a failure? I also thought about doing something only one percent of people have done. That burning desire to be special kept me going that day as I wanted to quit.

I didn't stop once, and the marathon wasn't as bad as I thought. I was hoping when I crossed the finish line I would think, *Yay, I did it! I did something only one percent of people have ever done. People will think I'm a big deal now! All that hard work was worth it!* This wasn't the case. I remember thinking, *Is this it? It wasn't worth all this hard work.* I looked around and every other runner who crossed the finish line had smiles on their faces and loved ones congratulating them.

Every runner had people who were there for them. I was the only one with no cheerleading section. It was the saddest moment of my life. I realized people didn't show up for me because I wasn't showing up for them. I was so wrapped up trying to be significant that I forgot what matters most, your relationships. This experience served as a warning to change my ways.

Maybe you're not the top one percent in something, but you could be if you put 100 percent of your focus towards it and neglected every other part of your life. You may reach the proverbial finish line, but how good will you feel if you don't have anyone there with you? How good will you feel if you have no one to run the race with you?

Every year at Christmas, my family watches *A Christmas Carol* and the message is the same as my marathon story. There's more to life than excelling at something; what's more important is being there for other people, and having a positive effect on them. We don't usually get the opportunity to have the ghost of Christmas past, present, and future visit us and help us change our ways, but just because something happens to someone else doesn't mean we can't learn from it, too.

In a way, because I thought so deeply about running that marathon, and based on how empty I felt after crossing the finish line, it served as a *Christmas Carol* moment for me. I had to change my ways or I risked spending a life in constant pursuit of significance, yet always feeling empty.

I would say that you have to give up excelling at something, but I've learned from experience that's not your solution. I spent a couple months not having any goals, not pursuing any dreams, and just trying to have fun with others, and I got tired of that real quick. Life becomes an exciting adventure when you work on dreams that cause you to get up early and stay up late. You don't have to give them up. You just have to make sure you make room in your life for others, too.

Shawn Achor, author of one of my favorite books, *The Happiness Advantage*, says, "Your social capital is the most valuable asset you have in terms of your happiness." To sum up what I learned from this marathon story: you can strive to be significant in some areas, but make sure you're significant in the lives of those around you as well.

They will be able to cheer you on as you work on your dreams and you can cheer them on as they go for theirs. You'd have people to support you in tough times when you want to give up, and whether or not you make it big, whether you cross this finish line or not, your life will have significance. Maybe you're not in the top one percent of something, but people who know you will say you were a person who always made the time to help them, care for them, and be present in their lives. When you think about it, what's more significant than that?

CHAPTER 15

BEAUTY INSPIRES

When you're around people you're comfortable with, amazing things can happen. You can take your mask off; you can be open and real. One day in college, at a pizza place, my friends and I were talking about the effect pretty women had on us. One said something like, "I can't believe I watched *The Notebook* last night. I hate romantic stuff like that, but my girlfriend's beauty has that effect over me." Another friend said, "I hate college, but I know women want an educated man."

What they were saying was resonating so strongly with me. I said everything I was thinking, starting with, "Guys, if there were no women on the planet, I would not be in college. I'd be driving my '95 Mercury Sable for the rest of my life. I'd live with my parents. I probably wouldn't shower. I wouldn't wear deodorant, brush my teeth, or comb my hair." I was just getting warmed up, but I had to stop because my friends were laughing so much.

I wasn't trying to be funny, though. A majority of my motivation and inspiration came from winning the heart of a beautiful woman. We go above and beyond at times to acquire what we consider beauty; that could be something like money, or success, or someone.

In my first year of college I had a crush on a girl we'll refer to as Chloe. She had piercing blue eyes, porcelain skin, and was emotionally deep. One of the first things I saw on her Facebook page was a quote that said, "To the world you may be one person, but to one person you may be the world." *What a catch!*

During this time in 2009 the *Twilight* vampire movies were incredibly popular. New Moon, the second movie in the series, had just came out. Chloe routinely mentioned how muscular and ripped Taylor Lautner, the actor who played werewolf Jacob Black, was. I thought, *the solution is simple; just get ripped like that guy, and Chloe will be with me.*

I was inspired to start weight training, drinking raw eggs, and eating as much chicken I could get my hands on. Over the next 6 months I had put on 20 pounds of lean weight and felt I was looking a lot like the guy Chloe desired. I was inspired by her beauty. But all my hard work in the gym didn't change much; she still saw me as just a smart guy who could help her with her chemistry homework.

This pattern carried on for the next ten years. I would be motivated and inspired to impress a girl I was pursuing or dating. But when the relationship didn't work out I'd find myself in a rut. Recently, I was in the rut for a couple months: I didn't have a beautiful woman in my life to inspire me.

After deep thought, it seemed it was time to be inspired by a different type of beauty. We all are inspired by beauty, whether it be a potential mate, art, music, or whatever else is coming to your mind at this moment. Your vision for your future can inspire you; maybe you close your eyes and you have a chiseled physique, you're wealthy beyond your wildest imagination, or you have the perfect romance.

That beautiful vision for your future can inspire you to go to the gym before work, invest and save, or possibly spend four hours typing up a three paragraph sales pitch on why you're the perfect man or woman on match.com. Beauty inspires. The problem is the type of beauty we are being inspired by. It's all on the surface. Physical beauty fades, the beautiful possessions that come from having money lose their value, and people seem to fall in and out of love all the time.

It's okay to be inspired by beauty. But to have sustainable inspiration, you need to look at the other side of beauty. The inside. I realized I didn't need a beautiful woman. I just needed to start looking for a different kind of beauty by which to be inspired.

It's so true what the late Dr. Wayne Dyer said: "When you change the way you look at things, the things you look at change." I had recently started going to a church over the past couple months, hoping to find answers to the deep questions I had, and looking to have a more meaningful life.

Stephen, the pastor at that church, is extremely friendly, who smiles so much it likely hurts his face. It seemed random, but he reached out to me and wanted to meet with me for dinner one Thursday night. I wasn't entirely sure what it was about, because at the end of service one day he asked me to hold a sign directing guests to sign up for a class, but I hardly thought doing a job a stand could do deserved a dinner.

I went hoping to help this man in whatever way he needed. However, he ended up helping me find the type of beauty that could inspire you for the rest of your life. He talked about how his faith changed his motivation in life. Years ago before he worked at the church, he was a welder, and apparently was a rock star at what he did.

He was so skilled that other companies were taking notice and trying to recruit him. At the time, his wife was months away from giving birth to their child and they were strapped for money. A rival company reached out to him and was offering him a salary much higher than his current job. If you were offered a job at a rival company for a large increase in salary, would you take it?

Stephen went up to his boss and said, "Another company is offering me a job at a salary significantly higher than what I'm making here. I'm happy working here, and I'm not asking for you to match their offer but I wanted to let you know I do plan on meeting with this company because I want to be honest and not do this behind your back."

Once again, he could have really used that extra income to support his growing family, but he used his leverage in a way most people don't. His boss said, "Stephen, you're my top guy. I can't afford to lose you. What will it take to keep you here?"

Stephen mentioned to me that his boss and his boss's family had never taken him up on his offer to visit his church, but despite all the times they declined he decided to ask one more time.

He said to his boss, "Tell you what, if you and your family come to my church the next three weeks, I'll stay here and I won't even go explore that job offer." "Done!" his boss exclaimed. He was worried his wife and family wouldn't be on board, but Stephen was such a good worker, he couldn't lose him.

His boss held up his end of the deal and went to church with his family those three weeks. Stephen held up his end and stayed at that company for a year until he left to work at the church permanently. His boss' family now goes to church on a regular basis and they're grateful Stephen persuaded them to come.

What Stephen did was the beauty I believe I have been seeking all these years. Regardless if you're religious or not, think about the position Stephen was in. He had all the leverage. He could have looked out for what was best for him and his family and gone with that other high-paying job. He also could have leveraged a higher salary at his current job or demanded perks such as an easier work schedule or his own parking space.

Here he was in a position to make *his* life better, and his focus was on helping his boss on what he believed he was lacking in his life. I was incredibly inspired by this story Stephen shared me with and it made me want to be more like him. You see, I believe I've been so inspired by pretty women because that's something that has been lacking in my life.

Many have inspiration that comes from what is lacking *in their own* life. Stephen's inspiration was coming from what was lacking in the lives of others. What if you gave your best effort in whatever you did, not to receive benefits that lead to a more comfortable life for yourself, but to develop your character and comfort the lives of those around you?

As your character develops, you'll stand out and be given opportunities. What if you use those opportunities to help others instead of yourself? I think of this fable of the man and the priceless stone. The man has found a diamond the size of a grapefruit. He could easily cash it in and be set for life. He could live like a king. Walking down the street, he sees a poor man seeking money for food and clothing.

For reasons most of us can't comprehend, the man hands over the priceless stone and says, "Use this, go get what you need." He walks off, not even expecting a thank you from the poor man. In complete amazement, the poor man is staring at the stone and thinks, *I thought a stone like this is all I ever wanted, but now I want something far more meaningful. I want whatever was in that man to give a priceless stone like this to a complete stranger.*

Could it be that we're failing to see the beauty that no one notices? Could we be valuing the wrong things? I heard years ago that the day before a Black Friday, a couple people broke into the store and switched the price tags of everything. $500 plasma TVs were now $5, and $5 underwear was now $500.

Maybe the price tags have been switched on what we consider beautiful and desirable and it's time to switch them back. Physical beauty fades, the value of that sports car you want will fade, those accomplishments you've made will be outshined by others who've accomplished them in less time.

The value of high character increases over time, and the beauty that comes from helping others is *never* going to fade. It does seem risky to make this shift, to start valuing being a person of character and being a person who uses your influence to comfort others instead of yourself.

It's worth considering, because the beauty that comes from living a life like this inspires you more than ever before. It will lead you to becoming abundantly blessed. Proverbs 11:25 MSG says, "Those who bless others are abundantly blessed; Those who help others are helped."

For example, years ago I was watching *Parks and Recreation*, a hilarious sitcom starring Amy Poehler, who plays Leslie Knope. Leslie runs the parks department and she's incredibly passionate about what she does, and always seems to be there for other people.

In one episode Leslie needs to ask the police chief for a favor, to have the police provide security for an event the parks department has a small budget for. She's already asked him for a favor and she's nervous about asking for more help. She can't be at the meeting, so she sends coworker, Ben Wyatt, instead.

When Ben arrives at the police station to ask for the favor, he's starts saying what Leslie coached him to say, but the police chief immediately interrupts him, agrees to the favor, and says Leslie Knope can have as many favors as she wants. Completely shocked and confused, Ben asks why he said yes. The police chief replies,

"Because when Leslie asks for a favor, it's always to help someone else."

People will protect you and look out for you when they know you're looking out for them. I've given you a real life example from the pastor of my church. He's one of the happiest guys I know. I've also shared a fictional example, from *Parks and Recreation*. Both have the type of beauty that can inspire for the right reasons.

I'm learning that the most inspiring people are not necessarily the most physically attractive, financially wealthy, or the most famous. The most inspiring people have their beauty from the inside, which gets displayed through their character and their focus on helping others.

One hypothetical question to assess where you stand is this: a genie pops out of a magic lamp and gives you three wishes. If those three wishes were granted, would the world change for the better, or just *your life?*

Ever since that meeting with Stephen, I've been thinking about the story he shared. I feel more inspired than ever. It's the kind of story that makes you want to build a good name for yourself, generate opportunities, and use those opportunities to help others. It makes you want to be more open and honest and share details of your life that aren't the most flattering, such as when I said I wouldn't wear deodorant if no women were present. Your mind and heart will change for the better once you're inspired by the right type of beauty; the beauty that seeks to enrich the lives of those around you. This kind of beauty can change your ways. I now wear deodorant *all the time* now just in case you were wondering. Is it time for you to change your ways, too?

CHAPTER 16

SETTLING ON THE EASY LEVEL

I just finished performing in front of thousands of screaming fans. I received a standing ovation and everyone was chanting for an encore. *Wow! It turns out I have a gift after all!* This moment happened when I was 19.

On a Thursday night at 9:30 p.m., I was playing *Guitar Hero 3: Legends of Rock* in Walmart. This video game is like *Dance Dance Revolution* but with a guitar. In this game players use a guitar-shaped game controller to simulate playing several types of guitars across numerous rock music songs. Players match notes that scroll on-screen to colored fret buttons on the controller, hitting the right notes keeps the virtual audience excited.

When you're hitting your notes, the virtual crowd in the game goes wild, but when you miss them, you get booed. Miss too many notes and your cord gets ripped off from your guitar and you're booed off stage before you get to complete your song.

The first song I played on this game was "Slow Ride" by Foghat. The character I choose to select was "Johnny Napalm," a punk rocker with a giant, green mohawk. I really did feel like a rock star once the song was over, I didn't miss a single note and during the song the virtual crowd in the video game was cheering me on, begging for an encore. At that current time in my young life, it was my proudest moment. Sad, but true. I was strutting around that video game section with my chest puffed out and walking three inches taller.

Unfortunately, there was only one person to witness my exceptional play, my 16-year-old sister. She immediately tried to humble me, "Michael, sorry to break this to you but you shouldn't be bragging. you're playing on the easy level."

This was almost a decade ago and there's so much we can learn from it. We all play the easy level at times and stay in our comfort zone. This chapter will offer insights on how you can grow as a person and play on the highest level in life. It starts with a push, and this is often from another person. My sister was pushing me to move up a level. Too many times we're so blinded by our doubts that we can't see ourselves moving to another level.

Plus, we don't like being pushed. We often associate it with a negative experience. Maybe it was a bully pushing you into lockers in high school, or maybe you can think of times when you were peer pressured to drink or smoke because it was "what the cool kids were doing". These examples are clearly negative. They are pushes away from being your best self. Pushes can be positive though. My sister pushing me that Thursday night was to help me become a better virtual guitarist. She didn't want a potential rock star to stay on the easy level.

We also have friends and family who push us to act when we're afraid of failing. There is one person who has a crush on someone they work with, go to school with, live near etc, and they tell their friend all about them. How he's a total stud muffin, or how she's a beautiful angel, but they never have the courage to talk to them and ask them out. Then one day a friend pushes you by saying, "Stop being a coward and go talk to them. Ask for her number. Ask for a date. Do you really want to wonder *what if?* your whole life?" When you're pushed to a new level, uncertainty is introduced. And you may not get the results you want right away. You may be tempted to stay where you are and tell your friend you don't care that they think you're a coward, even though you secretly do.

That night in Walmart, I wanted to stay on the easy level. On the easy level, notes scroll across the screen slowly and you only have to focus on hitting three out of the five fret buttons on your controller; the red, yellow, and green buttons. You don't have to worry about the orange and blue ones.

Moving up to the next level was a huge risk for me. I was a rock star at the easy level. *What if I move up to the medium level and I get booed off stage? What if I move to the medium level and it turns out I'm no rockstar after all, but only ordinary like in every other area of my life?* This is why so many of us would rather visit the perfect fantasy in our imagination, as opposed to taking the steps to make that fantasy a reality.

I decided to give the next level a try. It was just a game, and I had nothing to lose. I played "Slow Ride" again but I was not having fun this time. The notes were flying across the screen at twice the speed and I was now responsible for four out of the five fret buttons. The virtual audience thought I was a gifted guitarist on the easy level, but with each missed note on the medium level the crowd's groans grew.

I was halfway through the song before the music stopped and I was booed off the virtual stage. It was just a game, so why was I on the verge of tears? It's because I was thinking deeper than just a game. I was thinking that this is how life is.

In order to do something great with your life, you have to challenge yourself, and move up to the next level, even when you're filled with doubt and paralyzed by fear. Just minutes prior I was feeling euphoric, believing I was a guitar hero prodigy, but now I felt deflated. If I'm being honest, I've handled failure the wrong way most of my life. After that night, because I was booed off stage, I never wanted to play Guitar Hero again.

Months later, I asked out a girl I worked with after weeks of being pushed by my Dad and best friend, Ben. "Uh hey, Sarah, uh, uh. I'm not sure what you are doing this weekend, but if you're free, maybe we could, um go to the movies or something. If you don't want to, that's cool, I just wanted to ask because I thought that maybe you would want to like uh do something."

"Michael, thanks, but no thanks." *Ouch!* If I would have gotten a yes I would have hugged my dad and best friend and said, "Thanks, guys, for pushing me. I wouldn't have had the courage to do it without you." But when it doesn't work out it's a different story. "See, I told you she'd say no. Now the whole school is going to find out and make fun of me. This is why I didn't want to ask. I'm never asking out another girl again!"

The biggest mistake we make is that we think the first failed attempt defines us. You see, since Sarah rejected me I just assumed all the women on the planet would reject me as well. Four years went by before I asked out another woman. What helped me try again is what I learned from Zig Ziglar, that "failure is an event, not a person".

Sure, I failed on the medium level in Guitar Hero; sure, I struck out with that cashier at the grocery store I had a crush on, but these things can't make you a failure as a person. We stay on the easy level in life because we take failure too personally. We can grasp this, but still not try again, because we worry about what others think.

In my first year of college, in Psychology 101, I found another piece of the puzzle when I learned about the "Spotlight Effect." This refers to the tendency to think that more people notice something about you than they really do. We think others are obsessed with us, having the spotlight on us, when they likely aren't thinking about you at all.

Dale Carnegie, author of the book *How to Win Friends and Influence People,* asked his readers who is the first person they look at when they're in a group photo. I look at myself. I'm sure you do too. Let this free you. People are so consumed with what others think of them that they won't be thinking about you and your failures.

I thought when Sarah got off her shift, she picked up the phone and told her whole contact list, "You won't believe who asked me out this weekend. Michael." I thought this one event was going to be the focus of her life for years. How silly is this? If you want to play on the highest level in life, and do something rock star worthy, you're going to have to be willing to fail in front of others.

We are so afraid of failing because that event is like a snapshot of our lives, and we may believe it's the only snapshot people will ever see, i.e. it will define us. That might be why most of us try so hard to show only beautiful shots of ourselves on Instagram and Facebook. We want these success shots to define us, so that we feel better about ourselves in some way. But life is not a snapshot, it's a moving picture. Plus, people are too wrapped up in showcasing *their own* snapshots to be focusing on *yours.*

Just to make a point to myself, a few months back I intentionally took the most grotesque photo I could. Poor lighting, a terrible angle where I had a double chin, and the most unattractive facial gesture I could muster. It took me 11 selfies to get the photo I wanted. I then put the picture up on Instagram and Facebook for all my closest family and friends to see, with this text added:

"It seems like we're all trying so hard to showcase our best pictures on social media, but we still aren't satisfied in life. What if you did the opposite? Share the worst picture of yourself you can find. You may find that it frees you. If you're willing to let people see you at your worst, you don't have to obsess at people seeing you at your best. I dare you to share your worst picture."

The result? It didn't kill me. Somehow, the world was able to keep spinning with my grotesque photo out for everyone to see. It was freeing to me. Plus, it was cool to see a handful of my friends share a bad photo, too. Theirs were pretty bad, but mine was by far the worst. *Strangest competition ever.* This little experiment proved my point that people aren't focusing on you as much as you think they are. Also, when you have people in your life who love and accept the real you, both your good and bad pictures, you'll be less likely to obsess over sharing your perfect snapshots with strangers that display yourself in a light brighter than you really are.

Even though I knew I could start trying and failing and I'd be okay, I *still* delayed action. I had gotten used to living in my comfort zone. I wanted to write a book, but sitting down to write was harder than staying in my bed, wearing sweatpants, and watching *Seinfeld* reruns all day. On the easy level, I didn't have to push myself. I didn't have to be uncomfortable. But then a Seinfeld episode spoke to me.

The *Seinfeld* episode, titled "The Foundation", helped me realize how foolish you look staying on the easy level in anything. In this episode we learn that Elaine's boss just ran off to Myanmar, and has left Elaine in charge of running the catalog. This is a level up for Elaine, and whenever this happens in life you doubt yourself and wonder if you can even do it. Elaine is voicing her doubts to Jerry, "I am not qualified to run the catalog." Jerry agrees with her.

Jerry is no source of encouragement to Elaine, but Kramer barges into Jerry's apartment in time to hear Elaine say, "I'm just going to tell him no I can't run the catalog." "Woah! Can't? When did that word enter your vocabulary?" Kramer exclaims and continues. "When I first started karate, I had no support. The first time I sparred with an opponent I was terrified! Then I found my katra, your spirit, your being, the part of you that says, yes I can! So I listened to my katra, now I'm dominating the dojo, I'm class champion," Kramer says with a similar sense of pride I felt after playing the easy level on Guitar Hero perfectly.

Elaine is moved by Kramer's encouraging karate story and decides to accept the challenge and run the catalog, leaving Jerry's apartment to get to work. At this point a nine-year-old kid in a white karate outfit and yellow belt tied around his waist barges through the door, "Come on, Kramer! My mom is down in the car."

With confusion Jerry asks, "You guys both have class at the same time?" "We're in the same class," Kramer replies. "What do you mean you're in the same class?" Jerry fires back. "He almost beat me!" admits Kramer. "Kramer, you're fighting children!" "We're on the same skill level, Jerry!"

Later on in the episode, a 30-second clip shows Kramer sparring one-on-one with nine year olds and defeating them all with ease. It was absurd and hilarious, until I realized I had been doing the exact same thing as Kramer: fighting proverbial kids in my life. Maybe you're doing the same thing, too. It occurred to me that when we aren't excelling in life, we may seek an easier level so that we feel better about ourselves.

Whenever you're offered an opportunity to move up a level in life, like Elaine did with running the catalog, and you decide to stay on the easy level for fear of failure, fear of being booed, or fear of being average, you're like Kramer, a 6'3 grown man fighting nine-year-olds or like me playing Guitar Hero on the easy level. Maybe you dominate at this level, but they are and always will be hollow victories.

Do you want the love of your life? You're going to have to ask them out and eventually profess your love to them, even though there's no guarantees of success. Do you want to write a book, start your own business, or switch careers? There's no guarantee it's going to work out, and you're almost certain to perform poorly in the early stages. Consider the alternative. If you *don't* take those risks to grow, you'll be like a 40-year-old fighting 9-year-olds. Your potential will far exceed the level you're living on. What is it going to take to avoid you being an underachieving "Kramer" in the dojo of life?

To add content to this chapter, I played Guitar Hero for a week. I decided to buy the game because it was on clearance at *Best Buy*. It may seem like a waste of time for a man in his mid-twenties to be playing Guitar Hero, but I wanted to prove I could perform above the easy level. I was looking to make this into a unique metaphor that we could apply to our lives.

Immediately I went straight to the medium level, and was booed by the virtual audience, but with a little more maturity I responded in a different way. *Don't move down to the easy level, that may help you feel better, but it never helps you become better.*

On the medium level there were more keys to hit and the notes were flying at a faster rate. I did get booed off stage about a dozen times, but I kept playing. Eventually those boos turned into cheers. I was mastering the medium level. Before I knew it, I pushed myself to move to the hard level. This new mindset was helping me level up.

This brings us to our final piece missing that's causing you to stay on the easy level. Love. I used to be terrified to do anything out of my comfort zone until I learned the truth of this verse, "There is no fear in love, but perfect love casts out fear..." -1 John 4:18

That's when I realized, when your dream is driven by love, love for others, love for the unique gifts you have to share, the fear goes away. When it's out of love, it's no longer about receiving cheers from others or them thinking you're a rock star. It's no longer, "What's in this for me?" but instead, "What's inside me for you?"

Love for what you're doing transcends the potentials for boos. It's all about becoming better to add more value to others. You see, you reaching your highest potential is a great service to your fellow man. It inspires them to be their best selves, and it will lead you to mastering your craft and contributing to the world in wonderful ways.

This truth has been helping me. I'm filled with doubt and fear. I think, *my stories are stupid. People are just going to laugh at me if I share them.* That's why I've spent years writing ideas down, but being too afraid to share them. Then love came into play. If these lessons enriched my life and turned my life around, wouldn't the rejection and criticism from 99 out of 100 people who read it be worth it if it helped *one* person? Of course it does. Love is taking the focus off you, and being pushed to do what you need to do to reach your highest level.

I'm not saying don't start on the easy level. You can start on the easy level to get the hang of the game, but don't live there for a false sense of confidence. Staying on the easy level robs you and others of your best self. Stop playing on the easy level to *feel* better and start leveling up to *become* better. Start playing on the level that's causing you to stretch. Do this and you may get booed today, but one day, your skills will be developed, and one day you won't be hearing virtual cheers from a video game, but experiencing the cheers from real people in real life.

You don't have to be a rock star today; just start doing what you can today to grow. Tell that special someone how you feel, or just starting talking to them. Apply for that promotion or fill out that application for that new job. You know what it is that you can be doing today that you've been putting off. I'll leave that specific action up to you. We are all counting on you to nurture the gift inside you to become a real life rock star. So we beg of you, stop settling for the easy level and level up!

CHAPTER 17

CONFIRM YOU'RE NOT A ROBOT

Think back to the last time you were purchasing something online. Before you could finalize your purchase, the reCaptcha box popped up on your screen. If you aren't familiar with this, it's a software that requires users to perform an action to confirm a human is accessing their site.

reCaptcha requires you to type in random letters, like one real example, "freitag Winnie". Other times you have a series of pictures and you have to select specific ones, such as the ones with cars or street signs. After you type in the phrase, or select the appropriate pictures, you then have to click the box that says, "I'm not a robot." Sometimes it's annoying when you have to keep typing new phrases in because the words are in some odd font you can't read, or choose another round of pictures because the cars or signs are harder to find than Waldo, but overall it's a good safety measure.

reCaptcha confirms you're a human being, but human beings can still be robotic. For example, what if you dress a certain way, not because you like it, but because that's what everyone else wears?

It's odd that online, constantly confirming you're human is a safety measure we highly encourage, but confirming you're human in real life is scary. This is because no two humans are alike, and unlike robots, we have the ability to think for ourselves, display emotion, and have a higher chance of making mistakes. It seems that when we're put in situations to confirm we're not a robot, we're not honest. We try to act human while remaining robotic.

Here's one example that happened to me. I was in a church small group that met every week. The host of the group mentioned to everyone that this is a safe place; you have the courage to take your mask off; you don't have to say your life is perfect when it isn't; you can be real. No one is here to judge you, we're just here to support you.

These people all knew each other well and had been doing this weekly meeting for over a year. This was brand new for me and I didn't know what to expect. The first question was, "What motivates you?" I was waiting for more to be added to it, but that was it. "What motivates you?" I was waiting for someone in the group to answer, but there was silence. It felt like a minute went by, and the silence was so awkward I had to say something.

"I'm motivated to help others and make the world a better place." It felt so good to break that awkward silence and everyone smiled and said, "That's great." I did go first, and I had never been in a meeting like this, but after hearing everyone else's answers I realized I had not taken off my mask. My answer displayed no vulnerability. One man in his twenties said that he's motivated by people being proud of him. He played football because it made his Dad proud, he got good grades in school because it made his mom proud, he put up shelving in his garage earlier that day in hopes of his wife saying she was proud of him. He was vulnerable and stated that what others think of him means more than what he thinks of himself.

Another woman grew up in Alabama and she carries a stigma about it, and is constantly trying to prove to other people how smart she is. Another man mentioned that he grew up poor and the kids teased him about it and he felt worthless.

He now is highly successful, but he admitted his motivation comes from avoiding the pain of being poor, that he buys things he doesn't need to impress others. In my imagination, I saw everyone else in that group take off their masks, be honest, and give an answer that put a green check on the box that confirmed they weren't robots. What's odd is that I could relate to almost everyone and their struggles, but I didn't have the courage to admit that. You see, I'm not used to confirming I'm not a robot. I'm used to showcasing how great my life is, and how successful I'm doing.

With most people, I would fit in, but on this Sunday night, I was the *only one* with the mask still on, I was the *only one* who had yet to confirm I was in fact human with flaws and imperfections. If I had heard everyone talk first, if I saw how open they were being, my answer would have been more like this: "I'm motivated to help others and make the world a better place...but a part of it is to avoid the pain of being selfish most of my life. I even recall one time while running a marathon and I was 23 miles in, and a volunteer held out two cups of water for myself and another man running the race. I didn't care about the other man. I grabbed both cups of water and drank them both, leaving the man dehydrated. On my birthday years ago, I was in great shape, was making good money, but I spent the day alone; no one was there for me. I realized I would have to change my ways and think about the needs of others if I was going to have people in my life."

That's an answer that confirms I'm not a robot. You see, I honestly do enjoy helping others, but that shift in my life came from from the pain of living selfishly. I understand being robotic when you're around people whose approval matters to you, but there's another side to being a robot. You can't be your true self, you can't reveal your insecurities and weaknesses.

A powerful realization came to me as I watched everyone that night confirm they weren't robots by being vulnerable. It's that when you allow yourself to be human, you allow yourself to be accepted not for who you think you should be, but for who *you really are*. Plus, when you do this, it gives people around you the courage to be human as well.

We may allow other people to program us like robots, to act, think, and feel a certain way, but you're not a robot. You're human. As the wise musician, Avril Lavigne, once sung in her smash hit, "Complicated", "Why do you have to make things so complicated? Actin' like somebody else, gets me frustrated." You're on this earth to be *you*, and that includes *your* imperfections.

Acting robotically is frustrating for all parties. For you, you constantly have to filter your thoughts and feelings about everything to make sure you're accepted. Also, when you're doing this, it forces the other person to do the same. I get you may have deeper insecurities, or things in your past that you're ashamed of, and it's harder to share them with everyone, but the more you accept them, the more you feel like you belong.

I came across one of the most powerful quotes I've heard in a long time from Author Bren'e Brown, "Because true belonging only happens when we present our authentic, imperfect selves to the world, our sense of belonging can never be greater than our level of self-acceptance."

All I'm saying is that you should make the effort to confirm you're not a robot. Be passionate about those things other people aren't passionate about. Stop trying to hide your quirks and imperfections; it's what makes you, you. It's the only way to truly belong.

It's so easy to *say* that you shouldn't worry about being approved of, that you should be real, but it's harder to *do*. You can take steps by looking for what I call, "Nickelback moments." It's bizarre what I've observed about the band Nickelback. They've sold millions of albums, they are incredibly popular, but I personally had not met a person who liked them. I would often hear people say that their music isn't true rock and roll and they are sellouts, but the truth is I enjoyed their music. Their songs, "How You Remind Me," "Savin' me", and "Hero" were some of my favorites.

If I was out running at 5 a.m. I would blast my iPod and sing along to Nickelback, but if I was lifting weights in the gym it was a different story. If I was around other guys who could possibly hear the music I was listening to I would make sure I wasn't listening to Nickelback. However, a friend of mine pointed out to me that I was a people pleaser and try too hard to get people to like me. I would have argued with him, but I didn't want him to be displeased with me. This realization led me to wanting to be more authentic. I had made a commitment that I was going to showcase my liking for Nickelback the next time I got the opportunity. Over the years I've had "confirm you're not a robot" moments where I was authentic and human. I've fused those moments together to create this story to illustrate how being authentic often plays out in your life

One week I was at the gym and Nickelback's "Rockstar" started booming. There were three guys who appeared to be working out together who were all more muscular than me. I've had shallow conversations with them and knew their names, but I would say we were more acquaintances than friends. One of them seemed displeased by the gym manager's music selection. "Ugh! Nickelback. They're the worst." The two other guys nodded in silent agreement. *This is it, this is your time, Michael. Time to face your fears, and be the real you.*

In a faint, cowardly voice I uttered, "Uh, I like Nickelback." "Sorry, what did you say, bro?" I took a deep breath and put more confidence behind my voice. "I like Nickelback. I have seven of their songs on my iPod. They're great to listen to. Nickelback gets so much hate, but I like them."

My heart was racing as I waited for the guys to tease me, but I was amazed by what happened. The man who made the negative comment paused and replied, "You know what. I like them too. They *do* have a lot of hits. I guess it's just popular to hate them and that's what I've been doing." The other two guys mentioned they liked Nickelback too and for a few minutes we talked about our favorite songs.

You see, I thought that I was going to get rejected for standing up and owning my liking of Nickelback, but it seemed to earn me *more* approval. If anything, these other guys were programmed to not like Nickelback because that's how the majority felt. That seems robotic to me, don't you think? This Nickelback story is a silly example, but it does illustrate how you gain more respect and approval standing up for something that other people don't believe in.

It could be something serious like politics, religion, or something not serious like Nickelback. Whatever it is, stand firm while showing respect towards other people. Have "Nickelback moments" to confirm you're not a robot. You'll be respected far more being human, not conforming to whatever the other person thinks or feels in order to be accepted. Are you a robot? Please confirm that you're human by being who you're on this earth to be.

CHAPTER 18

MAKE A U-TURN

I have had the following scenario play out with my mom several times over the years. She tells me about a new place to meet me, and I respond, "I'll be there. What's the address?" "Michael, you don't need the address, you just need to make a turn on...." I know it seems like I'm being a bad son, but when she's explaining the directions, I tune out. I wait until she is finishes and once again ask, "What's the address?" "Michael, you really need to know how to get around *without* a GPS. What if you're in a storm and the GPS isn't working due to poor reception?"

That is a risk I'm willing to take. Not *once* has my GPS ever not worked, even during snow storms and hurricanes. Why waste precious brain space remembering turns when your GPS remembers the turns for you, while also doing it in the fastest way possible?

My GPS has been one of my prized possessions over the years, but a few months back I wanted to throw it out the window. I was coming back from visiting my parents in Myrtle Beach. I had made this drive dozens of times, but turned on my GPS because it was past 10 p.m. and too dark to see. Also, with the GPS guiding me I could focus a little more on the audiobook I was listening to, *The*

Happiness Advantage by Shawn Achor. A solid book worth checking out.

I was on a back road that I took many times, but on this night, the woman's voice on my GPS was saying, "Make a U-turn." I had taken this road dozens of times and it had *always* gotten me home. I ignored my GPS. Every time I had an opportunity to turn around, my GPS would say, "Make a U-Turn."

I drove down this road for another five minutes and must have heard another ten times, "Make a U-turn," and each time this happened the desire to chuck my GPS out the window increased. I didn't love the woman's voice on my GPS; I tolerated it because she always helped me get to where I needed to go.

However, on that night, my toleration for this voice had shifted to extreme annoyance, because it was telling me to go in a different direction when I was *certain* the way I was going was the right way. I went down this back road another five miles before realizing I should have trusted the voice of my GPS. This road was under construction and I had hit a dead end.

You see, my GPS knew that the path I was taking successfully all these years would not work for this trip. It was still guiding me to where I needed to go in the fastest way possible, I just didn't trust it. I believe one day we all have moments like I had that night. We've been living a certain way most of our lives, but something inside us is prompting us, "Make a U-Turn," but we may not be acting on it.

It could be that we don't make the turn because we don't like what a U-turn implies.

If you're told to make a U-turn in life, that means you're going in the wrong direction, you have to humble yourself, slow down, and head in the right direction. What if you've been going down one road your whole life, and now realize where you thought you wanted to go is not where you need to go?

I did my undergraduate schooling at a community college. It was a great school and I learned a lot, but the experience I had was not the college I envisioned. I thought I'd be in a fraternity, would attend wild parties, and have the time of my life. Instead, most of my classes were with adults twice my age. Let's play out a scenario of a man who is 35. We'll call him Kevin.

Kevin was my chemistry partner. In him I saw someone who was making a U-turn. He explained to me that growing up all he ever wanted to be was an architect. Playing with Legos was his thing as a kid, and he thought being an architect would allow him to feel like he was playing with Legos the rest of his life.

After high school, he took five years of schooling and got his Bachelor's in Architecture. He was an architect for a decade, but he found his life unsatisfying. He told me he was barely making enough to support his family and was consistently working 70-hour weeks. He would put his heart and soul into designing beautiful buildings, but they rarely came to life. His company wouldn't have the funding, or he would be told the designs are too impractical. Even though this man had a great attitude and outlook on life, the job he had was draining him.

Kevin' U-Turn would be changing careers. In order to do this, he would have to admit his dream wasn't what he wanted. He would have to let go of all the years and money he invested in becoming an architect. He would possibly have to spend another four years, and take out student loans to go in this new direction.

One day he woke up and realized being an architect wasn't what all that he had hoped and dreamed. His wife encouraged him to look into starting a new career. He researched a Physician's assistant. His income would be higher, he would be able to spend more time with his family, and he would be more fulfilled.

Kevin became a Physician Assistant. Years later, as he looks back, he believes he made the right choice. Kevin' story illustrates that the dreams we desire may not be what we hoped they would be. He also shows us that life changes drastically throughout our lives. Right out of high school, he wasn't thinking about the downsides of being an architect; that you may work more, get paid less, and never have your designs turned into buildings. He also wasn't thinking about the necessary quality time to spend with his wife and sons.

How easy would it be for him to think, *It's too late for me. I'm 35 and have kids. I've gone too far to turn around now.* Many of us do this. I worked with a 24-year-old who told me it was too late for her to go back to college. At 24, this person believed that all hope was lost for doing what she wanted to do.

When your priorities change and you find yourself going in a direction that's taking you away from what matters most to you, be willing to make a U-turn. Sometimes having a rock bottom moment can do this to you. Maybe it's getting fired, having a birthday that ends in zero or five, or maybe it's a picture.

A relative of mine recently started eating healthier and exercising. After a year of hard work, he looks great. I asked him what got him motivated to turn his health around. He said, "It wasn't until I saw a picture of myself on a recent family cruise. I was appalled by how I looked. "I looked like the bloated starfish, like Patrick Star from SpongeBob. That photo made me realize I had to do something *now*."

Notice that with both Kevin and my relative, they paused and evaluated their lives. They didn't like where they were heading and made a U-turn. Your career is important, and so is your physical health, but what about your mental, psychological, and spiritual health? What if you look like a bloated starfish *on the inside*?

Simply, make a U-turn. I think of a show I watched often years ago, *My Name is Earl*, that illustrates this. Earl Hickey, played by Jason Lee, is a small-time thief, living in the fictional rural town of Camden, who loses his winning $100,000 lottery ticket after being hit by a car while he celebrates his good fortune. Lying in a hospital bed, he learns about karma during an episode of the talk show *Last Call with Carson Daly*.

Convinced he has to turn his life around to be happy, Earl gives himself over to the power of karma. He makes a list of every bad thing and every person he has ever wronged and makes efforts to fix them all. After doing a first good deed, he finds the $100,000 lottery ticket that he had lost. Seeing this as a sign of karma rewarding him for his commitment, Earl uses his newfound wealth to do more good deeds according to his list.

The show had 96 episodes and after watching many of them several times, it inspired me to make changes for the better. I got picked on in high school, but if I'm being honest I do remember a time where I picked on someone: Blake. In middle school my mom bought me some Ralph Lauren polo shirts at the discount department store, *Ross*, and I was feeling superior compared to Blake's ragged clothes.

There were about ten kids around me when I started ragging Blake about his clothes. Everyone was laughing. Except Blake. I thought not being on the receiving end would make me feel good, but it didn't. For the rest of that year, every time I saw Blake I kept thinking, "Apologize to him." I heard it so many times to the point where I had to do something to silence it.

In hindsight, I tried to turn my conscience off. I gave myself excuses, "People have said mean things to you, and they never apologized, why should you?" "Kids say stupid things, he probably doesn't even remember what you said anyway," and "Apologizing is a sign a weakness, strong people don't do that." What excuses do you make to avoid doing what your conscience is telling you is right?

Years went by. I had received life lessons from *My Name is Earl*, and realized it was time to apologize to Blake. I was Facebook friends with him and typed out a lengthy Facebook message one day saying something along the lines of, "I know this is out of nowhere, but it's been bothering me for many years now. One day in middle school I was teasing you at lunch and don't even know if you remember it, but I do. I feel terrible about it, and hope it hasn't affected you in a negative way. I have no excuse to offer. I just wanted to apologize."

Later that afternoon, I saw that he read my comment, but never responded. I was hoping he would forgive me and say he didn't even remember it, but I'll never know. In the long run, I do believe good things happen to those who do what is right. However, I wouldn't bank on it. Sometimes the kindest people experience many misfortunes, and the cruelest seem to get many breaks. But it's the kind people who experience the most peace for doing what is right; they're the most successful on the inside.

Maybe when you try to do the right thing, your life doesn't change drastically on the outside, like it did for Earl getting that 100 grand-winning ticket back. But it can drastically change how you feel about yourself on the inside right away. It can silence your conscience because your actions are aligned with the person of character you aspire to be.

I share this example, because sometimes you're going to listen to your conscience and do what you believe is the right thing and not have karma reward you. Blake didn't forgive me and we didn't become best friends, but I finally had silenced my conscience on this event and my guilt went away.

We get internal "Make a U-Turn" promptings because our behavior is not in alignment with how we see ourselves, or how we want to be. This annoying voice that is your conscience wants you to be in congruence, where your values and beliefs are aligned with your actions.

That queasy feeling in your stomach when you're not listening to your conscience is just like that road I was traveling down a couple months ago. That feeling you have is telling you, "Make a U-turn."

Go say you're sorry. "Make a U-turn." You said you would be there at 7am, be there. "Make a U-turn." It's time to cut back on your spending. "Make a U-turn." It's time to cut ties with that toxic relationship. "Make a U-turn." It's time to start taking action today on your dreams and stop procrastinating.

Many of us try chuck our conscience out the window, and come up with reasons to make ourselves feel better. "No one ever apologized to me when they hurt my feelings so I'm not apologizing either." "No one honors their commitments anymore, plus it's crazy that they want me there at 7 a.m." "Everyone else is in debt, it's no big deal." "I know they are a bad influence on me, but they are so much fun." "I know I promised myself I would start working on my dream, but now's not the best time. I'll try next year."

It takes less effort on our part to shut off our conscience than to listen to it, but the relief is brief. Yes, in the present moment, we feel better, and maybe we don't feel guilty, but again, our conscience is not there to make our lives miserable, it's there to ensure we head down the right path and avoid the dead ends in life. With this strategy of shutting off our conscience, it's like me heading down that road that one night. We may be fine now, but one day it's going to lead to a dead end. It's never too late to turn your life around when you're willing to make a U-turn.

I *do* believe in taking directions from others who are wise and have been where you'd like to go. Most of my profound moments involved someone giving me advice on how to live differently, to make a U-turn when it came to my thoughts, feelings, or actions.

There's one mentor in my life I try to meet with once a month and almost every time I ask for his advice on something he'll ask, "Are you looking for validation or education?" He says that validation is all about what you *want* to hear. Education is what you *need* to hear.

Most of the time we want to hear that we're right and that we don't have to change anything. Like with me apologizing to Blake. If I was seeking validation, I would have kept asking people until I got the answer I wanted, "You don't have to apologize. You were a kid and everyone says and does things they don't mean." If I was seeking education I would have gotten advice that would have been truly helpful. "Stop looking for how everyone else would handle it. You know apologizing is the right thing. Go apologize now."

I've gotten a lot of great advice over the years, but advice that has been helping tremendously is that you have to get over being perfect. No matter how hard you try, you will slip up from time to time. When you slip up, be aware of your mistake and make a quick U-Turn to get back on the right path.

I used to diet and exercise intensely. Years ago, I would exercise every day, and I stuck to an eating plan that consisted mainly of grilled chicken and vegetables. I made the effort to follow this exercise and diet plan perfectly. But during the football season, I would slip up. On Sunday my family would often order pizza, wings, and have a bunch of tasty treats to indulge in while we watched the Miami Dolphins play.

All it would take is one bite of a chicken wing to make me think, *The day is ruined. You might as well eat 50 wings and a whole box of pizza.* That's what I did. Because I didn't eat perfect that day, I let go of all restriction and binge ate wings, pizza, ice cream, basically anything that was considered off limits with my diet.

I ate so much that it would often take a full week of exercising and eating right just to make up for the weight I gained on the day of binging. Several people told me my diet and eating plan was unrealistic and that I couldn't expect to follow it the rest of my life. I had come to terms with that and allowed myself every once in a while to have a "cheat meal" that was in moderation, such as two slices of pizza and a handful of wings.

Also, if something unexpected came up and I didn't have time to exercise, I would just let that day go. The result with this new approach to me eating and exercising? Less stress, more sanity, and it helped me get in the best shape of my life.

I tell you this because it's likely that you're too critical of yourself and guilt yourself too much when you slip up in life. Maybe it's letting your anger get the best of you and saying something hurtful you don't mean. Maybe it's getting too caught up with all your responsibilities and forgetting to get a relative a gift or failing to call someone you said you would.

I wouldn't advise scheduling a "cheat day" with your thinking and emotions, such as having a day where you get all the selfishness, anger, and forgetfulness out of your system. However, I would say that when you slip up and experience these days, do not let them derail you. Simply be aware of it when it's happening, stop it as soon as you can, and make it right with the other person if possible.

If the slip up is something you can't fix, learn from it and make the effort not to let it happen in the future. Here's an example in my life. Lately, I've been making the effort to write down three good things that happened in my day. It's advice I got from the book *The Happiness Advantage*. The author, Shawn Achor, sold me on the idea that we are products of what we focus on, that two people can be outside on a sunny day and one is happy because it's sunny, while the other is miserable because it's too hot.

Shawn writes that scanning the previous 24 hours for good things trains your brain to scan for the good things like the sunny part of the sun, instead of the heat. It doesn't have to be profound to be considered "good." It could be finding a funny YouTube video, getting a compliment from someone, or making small progress on one of your goals.

I did this "three good things" exercise every day for two months. I have a habit tracker app and my streak was up to 68 days in a row, but one day I forgot. The streak was broken. I was about to stop this daily habit since I'd have to start my steak all over again, but decided to make a U-Turn instead.

I thought, *You don't have to be perfect. You forgot to do this today, but don't let it derail you. Make a U-Turn, you can start up again and easily get back on track tomorrow.* That's all that day was, just a slip up. Plus, even with the slip up, that's 68 out of 69 days that I did do it, that's 98.6% of the time. Would you beat yourself up if you scored a 98.6 on your calculus test? I doubt it. Next time you have a slip up, do what I did and look at the big picture. When you see that a majority of times you succeed, the one tiny failure won't derail you.

The following day, I got back on track with my "three good things" routine, where I scan the past 24 hours and write three good things that happened to me. I believe you adopting this habit will dramatically improve your life. I know this example doesn't seem that big of a deal, but the way I approached the slip up certainly is. Whatever it is you're doing to improve your life and become a better person, don't let slip ups cause you to go in the wrong direction. Simply make the U-turn that takes you back to the right direction. Sometimes you need to score a 100%. For example, if you run a daycare center and take 50 kids to a water park, you can't lose one of them and say to the parent of the lost child, "We brought back 49 out of 50 kids back, that's 98%! We did an awesome job!" However, there are several scenarios in life, if you take a look at the big picture and look at the percentage of times you do something successfully, you'll be less likely to beat yourself up when you slip up.

We may have life-changing moments in our lives where we have to make a large scale decision like Kevin changing careers. We may have low moments like my relative seeing himself in a photo and looking like a bloated starfish. We may also have moments like Earl, where we realize we need to change our character to be happy. Or we could be on the right track in life, and slip up and feel lost from time to time.

We don't have to be perfect, and we don't have to have all the right answers in life now.

We just need to be willing to listen to our conscience, guiding us in the right direction and prompting us to make U-Turns when necessary. If we're willing to make these U-turns when we know we need to make them, we won't have to worry about hitting any dead ends in life.

CHAPTER 19

HUMBLE YOURSELF

When I was younger, I had one of the cheapest bikes Walmart had to offer. It wasn't a big deal.

Then one day it became one. I needed to impress twins in my neighborhood. Katie and Samantha. They had brown eyes, short brown bangs, and loved the Spice Girls. Katie and Samantha were two years older than me and out of my league. The only way I was going to win their hearts was to get a silver Mongoose BMX bike with pegs on the front and back. I needed the pegs so the three of us could go on our dates with one of the twins standing on the front pegs and the other on the back.

Christmas rolled around and my parents got me the bike. Unfortunately, to me, having the Mongoose bike *still* wasn't enough. I needed to take it up a notch. I needed to learn how to ride with no hands.

I never did ride my bike with no hands to impress these girls, and I never expressed how I felt about them or asked them out on a date. However, this is how I'd imagine it playing out if I did.

I would practice riding with no hands alone, where no one could see me fall. I would fall down *a lot*. But I would keep trying, because these girls were the loves of my life. They would be out dancing in their front yard singing along with the Spice Girls, "If you want to be my lover." And I would think, *Once you two watch me riding with no hands, you'll both be loving me.*"

I would be a few houses away riding closer and closer waiting until they were watching me. Once their eyes were on me, my hands would fly up in the air off the bike's handles.

Everything would be going as planned. I would be riding the bike with no hands. Their faces would be saying, "Wow, you're amazing, Michael." My face would say, "I know."

I would be so locked in on their reaction that I'd forget about the speed bump in front of their house. The speed bump would humble me. I'd fall right on my face. Before the fall the girls would ask: "Can you take us out, stud?" After the fall: "Do you want your mommy, little boy?"

Although this story played out in my imagination, this story has repeated itself time and time again in various ways throughout my life. It's a matter of pride. I was trying to elevate myself higher than I really was to impress these girls. What they thought of me caused me to ride dangerously. That speed bump was a stretch of road where I needed to grab my handles and ride in a non-flashy way to avoid the fall. But riding while holding onto the handles is not impressive, even though it prevents you from falling.

We all have stories like this where we are riding in life trying to do it with "no hands." With "no hands" living it's not about doing something in the most effective way, it's all about looking good doing it.

Maybe you're unhappy, in a lot of debt, or have problems that you can't solve on your own. These are like speed bumps. When you're about to hit a speed bump, do you humble yourself and ask for help? Do you humble yourself and admit it's too much to handle on your own? Do you humble yourself and admit your life isn't perfect like you project it to be on Instagram?

Proverbs 16:18 NIV says, "Pride goes before destruction, a haughty spirit before a fall." Being prideful and arrogant would have led to me trying to show off in front of those girls and it would have prevented me from seeing that speed bump. The only problem you may have is that you see many people who are prideful that seem to be succeeding in life. They're brilliant, famous, rich, have everything you want. They are "self-made." That term makes me laugh because no one is self-made. Your mom and dad were *literally* involved in making you. You had teachers, family, and friends who taught you values, and provided you support along the way. Even a person's enemies shape a person. They make you stronger, teach you about what you need to change, even if it's in a harmful way.

But every time you admit you don't know something, admit you're wrong, or admit you need help, that is like putting your hands on the handle bars. Your hands on the handlebars is you being humble.

Let's break this concept down and relate it to my botched attempt at winning the hearts of these older women with this verse, "For those who exalt themselves will be humbled, and those who humble themselves will be exalted." -Matthew 23:12 NLT

When you throw your hands up in life's journey and say, "Hey, check out how awesome I am," "I did it all by myself," "I have no weaknesses," "I have no problems," and "I'm better than you," these are all ways to exalt yourself. Sure, maybe for awhile, even for a stretch of years or decades, you seem unphased by exalting yourself, but life has a way of throwing unexpected speed bumps on these people, which lead to humiliations.

For me, trying to go through life with "no hands" has never worked. Has it worked for you? When you try to come across brilliant when you're not, you'll be humbled with a standardized test. When you try to come across rich when you're not, you'll be humbled when people find out you're in deep debt. When you tell everyone you are successful all because of your efforts alone, you'll be humbled when people who helped you along the way share the truth.

Imagine if you could let go of your pride and hold firmly to those handlebars. Imagine living a life where you had a purpose and a meaningful destination to travel that you didn't care how you got there. If you had to be humble the whole journey and ask for help and admit your weaknesses, but you would reach your destination, would it be worth it? I'd say yes. I'm learning that those who go the farthest in life also experience the most speed bumps. During these speed bumps, you have to have a firm handle and let go of your pride.

There's going to be someone out there that knows something you need to know. Humble yourself and let them teach you. There are going to be flaws and fears that you experience. Humble yourself and admit to yourself and others that you have them. There are going to be times where you're striving for something that's currently out of your league. Humble yourself through practice and patiently wait to develop.

The moment I humbled myself and revealed I wasn't perfect, and sought help for my problems, is the moment that speed bumps stopped causing me to fall. They slowed me down, yes, but didn't cause me to fall like that embarrassing daydream in front of Katie and Samantha. The moment you humble yourself is the moment you'll be exalted in life. You'll be *above* the need to win the approval of others, you'll be *above* the need to hide your imperfections from others, and you'll be done falling flat on your face.

Leave the "no hands" prideful lifestyle to those who are insecure and don't have a clear purpose for where they want to go in life. Be humble, grab on to whatever you need to get through the speed bumps, and go farther than you could ever imagine.

Maybe you're still not sold on being humble. How would you feel if you were the "low man on the totem pole"? I imagine you look at this in a negative way, as in, the low man on the totem pole in a company has an entry level job and is easily replaceable. You would take the necessary actions, even if it involves being prideful, to move up the totem.

What if I told you that you would do your most meaningful work while on the *bottom* of the proverbial totem pole? If you've ever seen an authentic totem they're often 30 to 40 feet high and often take several carvers. The most inexperienced carvers are assigned the top parts. This makes sense because most focus at their eye level when looking at a totem pole, which is near the bottom.

You see, the most skilled carvers are assigned to *the bottom* of the totem pole. If this is the case, why is the term "low man on the totem pole" considered insulting? I'm learning that if you are humble, never striving to prove how great you are or how you're better than others, this is the fastest way to rise in life. Saint Augustine realized this over 1,500 years ago when he said, "Do you wish to rise? Begin by *descending*. You plan a tower that will pierce the clouds? Lay first the foundation of humility."

Let's think about a human totem I was a part of growing up. When I was 13 my dad, my sister, and I would do something in the pool at our apartment complex that would turn heads. All three of us would go to the five-foot-deep water level of the pool and my 6'4" 230-pound dad would take a deep breath and squat down under water.

Then my 13-year-old, 5'2", 170-pound chubby self would climb on my dad's back, take a deep breath and squat as well. Then my 10-year-old, 90-pound sister would climb on my back with half of her body submerged under water. My dad would then straighten his legs and I would do the same. The longest time we were ever able to keep our 16-foot human totem upright, was 20 seconds. While we were upright in the pool, the four elderly women laying in the lounge chairs beside the pool gave us three golf claps for it.

Most would think the ideal place to be on this human totem would have been my sister's location. She was 10 feet above water and did not have to shoulder any weight. Although the top might be the most glamourous spot, it is the bottom that is most important. You see, my dad had to hold his breath the longest, waiting for my sister and I to climb on him, and he had to hold the most weight, 270 pounds between his two children.

Most people want to avoid the bottom position on the totem because it often takes more work, more responsibility, and often does not get the appreciation it deserves. However, this position makes you the strongest, and without building your strength, you can never become the person you're on this earth to be. It will take humility to become your strongest self. It will take humility to stop seeking the highest and easiest positions, and instead seek the lower ones that challenge you to develop.

Humility is something that many of us lack, and I can't speak for you, but for me it was challenging to be humble because I was lacking confidence, and my need for approval from others was too high. Any time I accomplished something, my mission was to tell everyone about it. Fortunately, I witnessed something during my first day of graduate school that made me value humility.

It was August in 2011 and I was starting my first year of graduate school at the Medical University of South Carolina. All the students from all the colleges of this school were gathered in an an auditorium that could fit over a thousand people. Students from medical, dental, nursing, physician assistant, and pharmacy schools were all present on this Friday morning for orientation.

There seemed to be about 600 students in this auditorium, but one person caught my eye. I was 20 feet from this man built like a Greek God. A Nigerian man who looked about 30, standing at 5'10 and weighing at least 220 pounds of solid muscle. His biceps were bigger than my head. That says a lot, because several people have mentioned how big my head is!

I didn't speak to him, but I read his name tag, Samkon Gado. *Hmm, why does that name sound so familiar?* I thought for 30 seconds while rubbing my chin. *Oh! I know how I know him! He was on my fantasy football team. He played running back in the National Football League and had a magical season in the second part of the 2005 season playing for the Green Bay Packers. He scored 7 touchdowns in 8 games!*

I was too giddy to talk to Samkon, giddier than I would be sitting on an airplane next to Taylor Swift. So, instead of approaching the man who helped me win my fantasy football league in 2005, I decided to tell a fellow pharmacy student sitting beside me, John, all about Samkon.

I tapped John on the shoulder and spoke softly so as not be rude and interrupt the dean who was speaking. "John, you see that gigantic muscular guy over there? That's Samkon Gado. He played in the NFL. Back in 2005 he was taking handoffs from Brett Favre and scored seven touchdowns in eight games." With a look of skepticism John responded, "Are you sure, Mike?" "No doubt about it, John."

At this time the dean said to us, "Over the next several years you'll become more acquainted with one another because you will need to work as a team to provide the best care to patients. Let's start getting to know each other. I'm going to hand someone the mic, and I'm going to ask you to give your name, what college you're in, and something interesting about you."

The dean handed the mic to a cute brunette in her early twenties, "I'm Courtney and I'm in the College of Dental Medicine, and I have a chocolate lab named Brownie." This was met with an audible "Awwwwww" by a quarter of the crowd, myself included.

Courtney then handed the mic to Samkon. *Wow, this is awesome. Samkon is going to reveal that he played in the NFL and now John will know I'm telling the truth. I won't have to convince anyone, because he's going to tell everyone now.*

Samkon's charming smile easily would put a smile on your face if you were there that day. He paused for a few seconds before saying something that is still etched in my mind many years later. "Hello, I'm Samkon Gado. I'm in the college of medicine." He then took a deep breath before continuing, "And something interesting about me is that I have 4 sisters." I was waiting for him to say, "And in 2005 during my rookie season in the NFL I came out of nowhere and scored 7 touchdowns for the Green Bay Packers."

Samkon said no such thing. It didn't make sense to me. If I was given the opportunity to brag about something in front of 600 people I would have done it in an extravagant way to make myself seem better than I really was. For example, the mic was never handed to me during orientation on that day, but I probably would have said. "I'm Michael, I'm in the College of Pharmacy, and I've done something only one percent of the world has done." Pausing for at least five seconds to build anticipation. "I ran a marathon."

I would have waited for a roaring applause. Would I mention the time it took me to run the marathon was embarrassingly long? Would I mention that a 60-year-old grandma, an 11-year-old boy, as well as hundreds of people running that marathon were faster than me? Of course not.

Later on, to prove to John that I was telling the truth, I had to show him Samkon's Wikipedia page, but I remember the rest of that day trying to process what Samkon did.

Samkon playing in the NFL was above and beyond anything I was expecting to do in my life, yet he was so humble and didn't have the need to share his accomplishments. Why did I have the need to tell everyone about my minor accomplishments, like my performance in

Mrs. Davidson's 5th grade class spelling bee? Or setting the high score for the basketball game in the local ice cream shop?

It was because Samkon had a character trait that I was lacking: humility. I finally tied deep meaning to a quote from a legendary Chicago Bear running back, Walter Payton, "When you're good at something, you'll tell everyone. When you're great at something, they'll tell you." I realized you tend to be prideful when your self-worth is tied into your accomplishments. When this is the case, you try to accomplish things you may not even care about. For example, I wasn't into running years ago, but when I heard that statistic of only 1 percent of the population running a marathon, I thought, *it may be a lot of hard work training for that, but to do something only 1 percent of people have done would make me special!*

What happened is that I devoted an incredible amount of effort training for that marathon *only* because I thought it could make me more significant. At best, when you are driven by what others think, you'll likely end up being considered "good". This is because when you waste time trying to brag and boast about what you've done, you don't spend time doing things that *truly* matter. You spend your time doing things making it *seem* to others that you matter.

I believe that you can become great, but in order for this to happen, you have to be humble. Don't be prideful like I've been. I've been trying to raise myself up for silly things like an elementary school spelling bee performance. Isn't it kind of pathetic that I would mention silly accomplishments like these to all the dates I had up until my mid-twenties?

I learning from my mistakes and I hope you do, too. When given the opportunity to showcase yourself like Samkon did during that orientation, don't lift yourself in pride, but remain grounded in humility. When you do this, people will raise you up and tell others how great you are like I'm doing now as I tell you about Samkon Gado.

Another benefit of having a firm grip on life's handle bars is that you benefit from others teaching you and helping you get more out of yourself than you ever would. You can have a beginner's mindset your entire life, always looking to learn and receive guidance from others no matter how successful you become. Can you remember a student in your class who would always ask the teacher 10,000 questions? Kind of annoying, right?

Some material in school was complex and wasn't easy to understand. Sometimes teachers teach material in a confusing way. Asking questions on how to explain it differently is necessary to grasp the material. I can think of many times when I was completely lost; I was even looking around and could see my other classmates were lost, and the teacher would say, "If you have any questions, please ask," but I would never ask.

Somebody! Anybody! Please ask the teacher to explain this in an easier way. I don't want to ask and have other people think I'm an idiot, I thought. When another student raised their hand and asked for clarification I sighed with relief, but if no one raised their hand and asked for clarification I thought, *Oh well. I guess if this material is on the test, I'm getting it wrong.*

I now realize how silly this logic is. I didn't want to *seem* like an idiot in front of my peers for admitting I didn't know something, so instead of asking a question to understand what confused me, I chose to remain lost. This seems like something an idiot does. Help is being offered to them, but they choose not to receive it because of pride.

This happened to me in Mr. Sheriff's calculus class in high school. It was the first advanced math class I had ever taken, and I was used to earning high A's in the regular math classes I had taken, but in this class I scored a C on the first test.

It seemed I was the only person that was lost in this class because the class average on that test was a 92 and Mr. Sheriff said this was the easiest test of the year. I remember vividly looking around during that second period in my junior year and hoping to find another student with an expression of confusion that I had, but no one did.

I was about to panic and try to drop out of the class, but then I realized how silly I was being. *Michael, you're not a genius, so what? Every other student understands this, but you don't. Humble yourself. Your teacher is asking if you have questions, and you have a bunch, stop being an idiot and settling for a C because you're too prideful and don't want to admit you need help.*

Looking back now, I became the low man on the totem pole in that calculus class. I accepted that I was likely the least intelligent student in the class. I accepted that I might need to study more, see the teacher after class for extra help, and ask questions during class.

On a Tuesday morning Mr. Sheriff was discussing integrals and derivatives. "This material is a little more challenging than what you've been learning so far, and I have no problem taking questions and re-explaining if anyone needs it," my teacher explained. Fifteen minutes into class Mr. Sheriff said, "Okay, does everyone understand this? Can we move on?"

Five seconds went by and I thought, *You don't understand, just raise your hand and ask.* My right hand was shaking, but I managed to raise it and say with a trembling voice, "Sir, I don't understand. Could you explain it again?" "Absolutely, Michael," Mr. Sheriff said with a smile.

My teacher explained the material a second time for me and all of a sudden it started making sense! I stopped being prideful and allowed myself to be helped. It was common for me to ask five questions per class period during the rest of that semester in that calculus class. I remember fellow students rolling their eyes and groaning with some questions I asked, but it's what I needed.

It's likely some students in my class thought, *Wow, this guy is an idiot*, but my grades were showing otherwise. I started excelling once I humbled myself. Fast forward to college, I had a 3.95 GPA.

Then in graduate school I was near the top of my class. My friend, I hope you know that I'm not trying to brag. I want to show you that if you're willing to humble yourself and ask for help, it can help you reach higher heights. From that first C in Mr. Sheriff's class in my junior year of high school, to graduating near the top of my class in graduate school, my IQ *did not* change. I just started using what I call the sling shot of humility.

I'm not going to say life is fair. At times people will have advantages that can take them farther in life, but they also may have a disadvantage that holds them back: pride. You see, some people go through life and people look at them in awe, "Wow, you're a natural," "Wow, you're gifted," "Wow, you're special." The downfall of this is at times these people will need help to move farther in life, but receiving help from others makes them less of a natural, less gifted, and less special in their eyes.

This fear of not being special prevents them from pulling back their pride and being humble. Someone who is humble pulls back their pride and receives all the help they need. When you humble yourself it's like using a sling. Think about someone who breaks their arm and has their arm in a sling. Do they appear weaker with the sling? Yes, but that sling helps them heal faster, which in the long run leads to them becoming stronger.

Now let's think about a slingshot. The farther you pull back a slingshot the more power you generate, and the farther the object can fly; the farther you pull back your pride, the more power *you* generate, and the farther *you* can fly.

You see, every time I went home and studied a couple more hours that the other students, every time I saw a teacher after class, and every time I asked a question in class, I was in a sling pulling myself back. Then when given the opportunity to test my power, I let go of the sling. Pulling back my pride and receiving help helped me fling farther than I could have ever imagined on my own.

You should have absolutely no problem receiving help because the more you allow yourself to be helped the more powerful you become, and the more powerful you become, the more you can help others.

Keep this in mind when you look at someone with envy. They may be smarter, more athletic, and more talented than you, but they likely have more pride than you, and they'll less likely to use that sling shot of humility. Keep this idea in mind, even when you're excelling. Always stay humble; you'll fly much farther in life when you do.

"But I don't want to be a burden to anyone by asking for their help," you may be thinking. I often wondered if teachers like Mr. Sheriff were bothered when they had students like me who asked for a ton of help, but their response has been unanimous. "It's because of students like you that make teaching so rewarding."

Isn't this the case for you? If someone values you and wants to learn from you, their appreciation for you makes you want to help them. Helping others can be incredibly rewarding and adds meaning to your life. Charles Dickens once said, "The flame of a candle is not diminished when it is used to light another." Using this quote and applying it to your life, wouldn't it make sense to pull back your pride, to be humble and let people light your candle to allow yourself to make the world a brighter place?

This is the longest chapter of the book and for good reason. I believe turning to the other side and going from pride to humility is one of the most crucial decisions you'll ever make in life. Pride will lead you to making a fool of yourself by trying to live with "no hands." This will cause you to fall flat on your face during life's speed bumps. Humility will allow you to grab onto life's handlebars.

Humility will lead you to moving past those speed bumps and keep moving forward.

Being humble will likely lead to me sharing your success story in a future book, as opposed to you bragging about it and having others think you're full of yourself. My friend, look on the other side of life with your pride. You'll find humility. Your greatest work will come from a heart of humility, and if you still feel something is missing in your life, you'll likely find it *after* you humble yourself.

CHAPTER 20

LET IT SINK IN

My sister lived with me at the time of this story. She buys almond milk and I've been tempted to try it for years now, but haven't for the longest time. "How does it taste?" I asked her a few weeks ago. "You're free to try it if you like, Bro." I held back from trying it because I had just brushed my teeth and knew the mintiness would negatively affect my first impression of the almond milk.

A couple days later I did take my sister up on her offer. The carton was basically empty, there seemed enough milk in the container to pour in a shot glass. I drank the milk straight from the carton and tossed it in the trash. For only having 30 calories per serving I thought it tasted fantastic. Later that night it turns out I made a mistake.

My sister got home late from work one night and opened the fridge and let out a groan. "Where's the almond milk?" "I had what was left of it, you said I could try it." "Well, you need to buy me a new carton," she exclaimed. "What?! I drank maybe two percent of the carton, that doesn't seem fair." "It is fair, Michael. Finishing the last two percent is worse than drinking the first 98 percent, because now I don't have any milk to drink." I didn't feel like arguing with her. So I just replaced the almond milk. This logic from my sister seemed silly at first, but after letting this sink in after weeks of reflection, I realize it's how most of us operate.

The ending of something is more important than the beginning or even the middle. For the most part, every movie you see ends with a happy ending. Every powerful story hits you with a moral that is memorable and forever changes your life. We all want to end on a high note. Whether it's a comedian finishing her set with her funniest joke and dropping the mic, or Peyton Manning winning the Superbowl and then retiring, we all want to leave on a high note.

I'm hoping to do the same with our time together. I've given a lot of consideration on how I wanted this book to end. It's to show you that looking on *The Other Side* of life is something worth doing *the rest of your life.*

I've demonstrated throughout our time together that it's okay to have flaws; it's what makes you human and not a robot. I've tried to show you that by working to address them by reflecting, looking on the other side of thoughts and events, that you would gather insights. Whether it be focusing on your smoke instead of your fire, or addressing your imaginary grizzly bears. These insights could help you learn from your mistakes and help you handle life better, and help you become a better person in the process.

The last lesson comes from how I was able to get the dirt off of my bathtub. For the most part, I like to consider myself a person who strives for excellence. I try to stay healthy and fit, I try to read on a daily basis, and work to be a more caring person. However, there's one area in my life that I didn't care about for the longest time; the cleanliness of my house.

I would have dozens of clothes just randomly laid on the floor in my bedroom to the point where you couldn't see the carpet. Food crumbs covered the couch and floor. But my bathtub was by far the worst. I had been living at that house two years and had not cleaned it *once*. Judge me if you want. It was disgusting. It started out white, but now the bottom floor was black with filth.

Then one day I made the effort to clean up my house. It all started when I was seeing this girl, Anastasia. What can I say? I was inspired by her beauty. I went from living like a slob for years to wanting to have the cleanest house in the world, all thanks to this pretty girl.

I scrubbed every toilet spotless, I vacuumed every square inch of my house. I even wanted to pull my fridge completely out to clean behind it.

I saved the toughest task for last. My bathtub. 98 percent of my house was clean, but the two percent remaining was going to be the hardest. The dirt seemed tattooed to that bathroom floor.

I bought a gallon of bleach, a scrub brush, and three dish rags to accomplish the task. I poured half the gallon of bleach and had the floor smothered. I then started scrubbing. I tried the scrub brush first. For several minutes I was brushing as hard as I could, to the point of sweating, but my effort seemed pointless. I then tried using rags. Once again, no luck. I spent twenty minutes honestly giving every ounce in me, before I had completely given up. I had accepted this dirt had sat on my bath floor for too long, and that it would remain there forever.

It was a Friday when I did all this cleaning in preparation for Anastasia coming the following day.

Anastasia and I talked on the phone a bit that Friday night and she could sense something was wrong. "What has you down, Michael?" "You won't believe this, but I have been cleaning all day. My house looks brand new. I know you said you don't care about how my house looks, but I wanted it spotless. But there's one spot I can't clean. The bathtub. I scrubbed it to the point of almost passing out, but it's *still* filthy!"

She asked how I was cleaning it and she realized my problem. "You're not letting the bleach sink in. Try it again, but this time pour the bleach and let it sit for 30 minutes before scrubbing." I said I'd try that, but was certain that wouldn't work. After all, I'm a strong man, and I put all my manly muscle into scrubbing that dirt and it wasn't coming off.

Like many times in life, we're trying to work harder, not smarter. Anastasia was absolutely right. After letting the bleach sink in for 30 minutes, I removed *all* the dirt from my bathtub with minimal scrubbing. I was convinced it was a miracle. I had been sure that the dirt was going to be there forever, but thanks to Anastasia's advice, I was able to remove it completely.

This tub story has a deeper lesson, and possibly carries more weight than the other ones. Letting bleach sink in before scrubbing helps you remove dirt from your tub with less effort. Letting information sink in before acting helps you remove bad choices and unwanted emotions with less effort. I have no problem admitting what I wrote in this book are likely concepts that you've already heard. You may not have heard it in the way I shared it, but the core of all the lessons you likely know.

You know that it's better to be kind instead of cruel, courageous instead of fearful, and generous instead of selfish. We've likely already heard what we need to hear in order to live our most fulfilling life, but why do we struggle to adopt it? I believe we're in such a rush to keep up with everyone else that we don't take the time to pause, we don't take time to let what happened to us *sink in*. Instead, we do like what I was doing, immediately trying to remove the dirt in our lives with brute force, instead of using the wiser, more effective approach.

I would love to tell you that this book is the end all be all, that after reading it your life will be as spotless as my bathtub, but it won't be. Being a human being implies that you're not perfect and never will be. Even though I've been advising you to be courageous, at times I act cowardly. Even though I've been advising you to look for what's best for others, at times I act selfishly.

The Other Side of life is about reflecting on the events in your life, the thoughts you're having and letting them sink in. It's about asking yourself questions you normally don't to ask. Such as, "What can I learn from this?" "How could I have handled this better?" and "Why am I acting the way I'm acting?"

In the shower this morning I couldn't help but realize dirt is starting to form, even with letting the bleach sink in. Just like in your life, even if you read hundreds of books, seek out wisdom from the wisest people on earth, and let it all sink in, you're *still* going to have dirt come into your life. This "dirt" could be letting fear get the best of you, saying something hurtful to someone who didn't deserve it, or any other negative thought or emotion that hinders you from living your best life.

It isn't wise to assume you're immune from this "dirt." I thought this was the case for me and it was a big mistake. Years ago, I started seeking advice from those wiser than me, reading on a daily basis, and even listening to audiobooks in the car. However, one day I thought, *I know enough, this stuff is common sense anyway*. It wasn't but a couple weeks until I went back to my old self, letting the dirt pile up in my life, and having a view of myself, others, and the world in a way that was negative and filthy.

I sincerely hope I've convinced you to start the process of seeking prosperity from your pain, lessons from your mistakes, and progress in a hopeless situation, but it will be an *ongoing* process. You see, you can be happy and fulfilled because of the *process* of looking at the other side of life, looking for breakthroughs and insights from every moment you can't see at first glance.

Just like my tub, your thoughts and emotions will only stay clean if you let information sink in *and* actively apply it the way you apply effort in scrubbing a tub. For the stories in this book, and anything else you hear in your life, let it sink in *first*, take the time to understand it completely, *then* apply it to your life.

When life's "dirt" comes, acknowledge it, pour some bleach over it (which could represent an empowering thought or story) let it sink it, take as long as you need to process it, then start scrubbing. When you're afraid, think about a story or quote that empowered you, let it sink it, then apply it to scrub the fear away. Carry on the same process with self-doubt, worry, or anything else that's hindering you.

I hope this last story ends our discussion on a high note and helps you realize there's another side of life you may have been missing, *The Other Side* you can start seeing today.

If there is anything in this book that helped you, or if you have questions for me, I'd love to hear from you!

If you are interested in having me speak about topics discussed in this book, you can reach me at:

Website: michaelunks.com
Email: unksmichael@gmail.com
YouTube: Michael Unks
Facebook: Michael Unks

Thanks again for reading this book, and hope it helps you see life more clearly!

Your friend,
Michael Unks

ACKNOWLEDGEMENTS

God: I have to thank You first. For my remaining days on earth, I want to represent You well and share the abundant love You've given me. The relationship I have with Your son, Jesus, is the most important one I have. In the morning I paraphrase Psalm 37:4 and tell You how I delight in You, and in doing so You give me the desires of my heart. My desire appears to be to use my words, enthusiasm, and unique perspective to enrich the lives of those around me.

My Family: I've always been able to count on you for your support. I admit I'm a "momma's boy," and every man would be one too if they had a mother as caring, loving, and supportive as you. Thank you for asking for a signed copy of this book when it was done. At least I know one person will be buying this! Love you, Mom. I *literally* wouldn't have done anything without you. Next, my stepdad, Don. Thank you for all your love and guidance over the years. Dad and my stepmom, Maria, thanks for all your love and encouragement. Grandma and Grandpap, thank you for thinking so highly of me and talking me up with all your square dance friends. Also, Grandma, thank you for all your help with my papers and books over the years. It has definitely helped me with writing this book. My youngest sister: You've repeatedly told me not to use your name in my book so I won't. But you know I'm talking to you and I want to thank you for your friendship over the years. My other sister, Blaine. You may be my biggest cheerleader. I think you've liked every video I've ever posted. Your support has kept me going over the years and I want you to know how grateful I am.

Dan Potter: When the draft of this book was done I was torn between three editors. I prayed about it, and it became clear you were the choice. I'm incredibly grateful for all your hard work on this book. Thanks to you, this book is grammatically correct and is no longer filled with a bunch of silly nonsense. Okay, maybe just a tad. You've become a great friend and I can't wait read all your best-selling books someday!

Ida Svenningson: Thank you for designing my cover. I can't get over how cool it looks. You're gifted at what you do!

Ron Collman: Thank you for your friendship and guidance over this past year. Many conversations we've had walking around your neighborhood will impact me for the rest of my life.

Phil Woody: Thank you for seeing something in me that I couldn't see myself. You've shared so many life lessons with me over the years and I hope you know how grateful I am to have you in my life.

Kurt Olson: It's unusual how we crossed paths in life, but I greatly value your encouragement and support over the years. Our "Sharpening Sessions" has led to many insights, some of which were put in this book. I highly value our friendship!

Ben Blevins: Thank you for being my best friend and supporting me in all I do. We had some incredible conversations over the years and I'm sure we'll have many more in the future.

Will Shealy: I truly believe you were my answered prayer when I asked God to send me someone to teach me how to change my ways. You've truly inspired me to serve others and I'm tremendously grateful for you persuading me to listen to Zig Ziglar.

Zig Ziglar: I'll never forget putting one of your motivational CDs in my car and listening to it. It radically transformed my life. I'll never forget the day I tried to contact you to thank you, but realized you passed away in 2012. I was devastated by this news and was wondering how I could repay you. I immediately had this feeling inside to find a way to impact someone else the way you impacted me. At times, I feel you're looking down from heaven encouraging me to keep going when I want to quit. I want to thank you. You were a great man and I've learned so much from you. Rest in peace knowing the tremendous impact you made on the world.

Chris Massey: Thank you for inviting me to Awaken and giving me a place where I feel like I belong. Also, thank you for inspiring me to be a better person.

Stephen Loadholdt: Thank you for serving as an example of how to be a follower of Christ. The love you have for people is inspiring, and I'm truly grateful for all the opportunities you have given me to serve at church.

Everyone at Awaken Church:

I'm getting a little nauseous because I already know I'm bound to leave someone out here. But thank you to everyone in leadership, including head Pastor Brandon Bowers. Your sermons have helped me to reflect deeply and see life more clearly. Also, anyone who serves at Awaken. You all have made Awaken an environment where people feel welcomed and loved. I'm grateful to be a part of it.

Oh, and I have to mention my small groups. To the Barton's, Collman's, Massey's, Floresca's, and Gaddy's, thank you for making me feel so welcome during our meetings on Sunday afternoon. Thank you for all your encouragement while in the process of writing this book.

Everyone in the "Skwadd" Small Group at Awaken

Nicole Hutchison, Chris and Chelsey Massey, Jacob Jourdain, Jared Matthews, Ben and Devynn Galloway, Rebecca Jackson, Molly Hartley, Ashleigh Watson, Jeremy Dickins and Cheyenne Banton. Thank you for being like family to me and allowing me to test out my material on you. Thanks to you, a lot of the bad ideas were cut out of this book.

Everyone at Publix Supermarket and Pharmacy

Since starting out as a bagboy at 14 to a Pharmacist as I write this today there have been so many people who have helped me become a better person. Shout out to the Goose Creek Pharmacy: Charity Macdowell, Dawn Thomas, Cindy Risso, Theresa Berry, Stephanie Rager, Louann Adams, Branden Capelton, Dillon Lewis, Josh Orara, and Amy Huynh. Thank you all for your hard work and helping me genuinely enjoy coming into work.

Again, thank you to anyone else not listed above. I wouldn't be where I am today if it wasn't for the people who have positively impacted my life.

If there is anything in this book that helped you, or if you have questions for me, I'd love to hear from you! Please reach out!

If you are interested in having me speak about topics discussed in this book, you can reach me at:

Website: michaelunks.com
Email: unksmichael@gmail.com
YouTube: Michael Unks
Facebook: Michael Unks

Thanks again for reading this book, and hope it helps you see life more clearly!

Your friend,
Michael Unks

Made in the USA
Middletown, DE
30 March 2023

Thank you for checking out this book.

I'm providing you the first five chapters of the audio version of this book for free.
Click the link below:

Send me the audio book

Also check out michaelunks.com for more free audio books!

I also have several book ideas. I can let you know when my next one comes out by clicking below:

Keep me posted

URGENT PLEA!

Thank You For Reading My Book!

I really appreciate all of your feedback, and I love hearing what you have to say.

I need your input to make the next version of this book and my future books even better.

Please leave me a helpful review on Amazon letting me know what you thought of the book.

Thank you so much!
~ Michael Unks